HORIZON READERS

UNKNOWN WAYS

MORE TALES OF EXPLORERS, PIONEERS AND TRAVELLERS

By

E. E. REYNOLDS

ILLUSTRATIONS BY S. TRESILIAN

Down the edges, through the passes, up the mountain steep,
Conquering, holding, daring, venturing, as we go the unknown ways,
Pioneers! O Pioneers!

WALT WHITMAN

T0345960

CAMBRIDGE
AT THE UNIVERSITY PRESS
1940

CAMBRIDGE UNIVERSITY PRESS
Cambridge, New York, Melbourne, Madrid, Cape Town,
Singapore, São Paulo, Delhi, Tokyo, Mexico City

Cambridge University Press
The Edinburgh Building, Cambridge CB2 8RU, UK

Published in the United States of America by
Cambridge University Press, New York

www.cambridge.org
Information on this title: www.cambridge.org/9781107600270

First published 1940
First paperback edition 2011

A catalogue record for this publication is available from the British Library

ISBN 978-1-107-60027-0 Paperback

CONTENTS

I

River Adventure

IT is difficult to believe that not much more than a hundred years ago the greater part of Australia was unexplored. The story of how that vast island was gradually opened-up to settlement is full of excitement, but here we are concerned only with one of the men who ventured 'behind the ranges'.

From the map you will see that there is a great mountain barrier at the south-east corner of Australia, the part now called New South Wales. The early settlements were round Botany Bay and the present Sydney; the fringe of coast between mountain and sea was first occupied.

What was behind that barrier? That was the question which those early pioneers asked themselves, and set out to answer.

Of them the boldest was Charles Sturt. He was an army Captain, but the rather humdrum life of a garrison officer bored him, and he was eager to find out what the interior of Australia was like.

His first great discovery was of the River Darling in 1829. He struck it much farther north than our map shows, but was unable at that time to trace it southwards.

A year later he set out from Sydney towards the south-west. It is the story of that expedition which I want to relate here.

Sturt started by following the river with the queer name of Murrumbidgee. At that time no one knew where the river went to, or how it reached the sea. It was a venture into the unknown. Sturt had a theory that it might join up with the Darling, and it was this theory which he wanted to test.

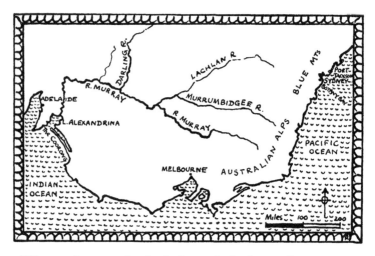

His equipment included a whale-boat (in sections) because he hoped to do part of the journey by river. The gear was carried on two drays and on pack horses.

They had not got far from the mountains before trouble began. They found a flat plain with scanty vegetation. The wheels of the wagons sank into the loamy clay and made every mile a tremendous labour.

At length Sturt decided that he must take to the river and send back his drays and horses. As a small boat would prove perhaps more useful than the whaler, they pitched camp and set to work building one. A suitable tree was felled and a saw-pit dug. Meantime the whale-boat was put together, and within seven days they had for their use both this larger vessel about twenty-seven feet long, and a smaller one half the length which they had built out of materials on the spot.

They stowed their gear and provisions (mostly salt pork) on board the two boats and set off down the river. The drays were sent back to Sydney. This was a bold decision, for a return journey on foot in such dreary country was, at the best, a risky business and might easily bring disaster. Sturt was really acting on the policy which Nansen always urged: cut off your own means of retreat and you must go forward since there is no going back. But it takes a brave man to make the decision.

The river took them along at a good pace, but the outlook was most depressing. The banks were lined with reeds; the explorers could seldom see more than three-quarters of a mile on either side over the flat country. The voyage was not without risks, for time and again they struck sunken rocks or even trees which had fallen into the water and had become as dangerous as the rocks.

There was the further danger of native attacks. The Australian blacks are some of the most primitive people in the world; they lead a hard life, and at that time few had seen a white man. It was therefore necessary to approach them carefully, and to win their friendship.

Some were met during the early part of the expedition, but when the clearer stretches of the river were reached, large tribes were seen along the banks.

At one point it looked as though there was real danger.

Towards evening, when the explorers were looking for a camp-site, a large party of natives appeared ahead of them on the right bank. Sturt did not wish for trouble, so he steered the boat towards the left bank. Almost immediately another party of blacks arrived on that side.

All carried spears which they beat on their shields and at the same time they let out terrifying shouts. Had both parties attacked at the same time they would have had the men in the boats at their mercy. It looked at first as though this was their plan, and Sturt got ready to put up a fight. He had no wish to shoot if it could be avoided, but just as he was about to give the order, the blacks on the left bank swam over and joined those on the right.

Sturt again took a bold decision. He ordered his men to pull into the left bank and pitch camp. Then he and his chief assistant, M'Leay, walked down to the river and held up branches to show that they wished for peace.

They could make their meaning clear only by means of such signs, but at last the blacks understood, and they put down their spears. Two or three started to swim across; the others tried to stop them but some followed.

As soon as the blacks landed, Sturt and M'Leay

walked away from the bank and sat down, that being the usual way of showing a wish to be friendly.

The natives came nearer and sat down and stared at the two white men. Sturt then gave them some presents, such as axes and pieces of hoop iron. This reassured the natives and they went along to look at the camp.

At dusk most of them went off, but three old men remained by the fire all night. M'Leay was able to get on good terms with them; he sang songs and laughed and put them into a good humour. The result was that when the camp was struck the next morning there were no signs of hostility, and the crowd of blacks watched the boats put off with every sign of friendliness. But it had been an anxious experience, and worse was to follow. Sturt felt that there could be little danger ahead as four of the natives followed them along the bank.

Now one problem in keeping to an unexplored river is that you do not know what lies ahead in the way of rocks and particularly of rapids. And it was this lack of information which almost wrecked the expedition.

The explorers had just followed a bend in the river when they saw ahead a foaming rapid. It was too late to retreat. All realised the danger and silence fell upon the party. Sturt stood up to get a better view of the course. He could make out a large rock standing almost in the middle of the river, with the water rushing down on either side. He could not see what lay beyond.

Quick decision was necessary, for the boats were

already in the pull of the current. Sturt tried to keep his boat in the most open water he could see. But a sunken rock defeated his scheme.

The keel struck the rocky ledge, and the boat swung round as if she were on a pivot. The small boat escaped and floated free.

Fortunately the rocks held the whaler, and the problem was to get her off without damage.

'Two of you get out with ropes', ordered Sturt.

There was a risk in this, for the lightening of the boat might mean that she would get loose while not under control.

Carefully two of the men got out on to the rock and by means of the ropes gradually worked the boat into calmer water and under the right bank. When they came to examine the boat they found very little damage. Had the rocks been more dangerous she might easily have been wrecked with all her valuable stores.

They pitched camp as soon as possible. The four natives again joined them and Sturt tried by sign-language to find out what kind of course the river followed.

With a number of sticks the natives made a rough diagram of the country, which at least served to show that the river followed a westerly direction.

The next day they made good progress, and after some nine miles they saw to their surprise that one bank was covered with great trees. So far they had only seen shrubs and dense undergrowth. As they drew nearer they found that a dense mass of blacks had collected on the bank amongst the trees.

They were singing a war-song and were all painted in various weird fashions. Some had marked their ribs and thighs with white so that they looked like walking skeletons; others were daubed over with red and yellow ochre, and their bodies shone with grease. All carried spears and shields and stood in menacing attitudes.

Sturt pulled out to mid-stream in the hope of avoiding a conflict. There was little risk of the natives hurling their spears at a moving target some distance from the bank. But they had not gone far before they saw that a long tongue of land ran down into the water from the bank, and the water began to get much more shallow.

The blacks rushed along the bank and massed themselves on the projecting land and there waited for the boats. It was clear that a conflict could no longer be avoided.

Sturt gave his orders, and handed out arms and ammunition.

'Our only chance', he said, 'is to be firm and cool. No one is to fire until I do. Shoot to frighten not to kill at first. They may be terrified at the first volley.'

Slowly the boat drew nearer the blacks. Sturt stood up and levelled his gun ready to fire. Just as he was about to do so, M'Leay called out, 'Look on the left bank. More of them!'

It was true. Another party of blacks had arrived on the other bank. There were not many of them, but their arrival seemed to take away all hope of a peaceful passage down the river.

Sturt lowered his gun. What was the use of firing it

now? But even while he paused in despair, a most unexpected thing happened.

One of the new arrivals leapt into the river and swam across to the main group of blacks. When he got to them he went up to one who seemed the chief, seized him by the throat and pushed him back from the bank. Then he began to shout at him. He shook his fist at the chief, then he pointed to the boat, stamped with passion and argued at the top of his voice.

Sturt could not understand what was being said, but by the black's signs and gestures it was clear that he was persuading the natives to let the white men pass uninjured.

So amazed were the explorers at this sudden turn of events, and their salvation from what seemed certain death, that they did not notice how the boats were drifting. They fetched up on a sandbank, and soon after getting off again they came to a new river flowing from the north.

This was an additional safeguard for it meant another stretch of water between them and their possible enemies. Sturt's thoughts immediately were busy with this fresh problem. Was this the Darling? He felt it must be and eventually he proved right. And the main river they were now on was to prove the great river of Australia, the Murray.

Meantime some of the friendly natives had swum across and waited on the far bank. Sturt decided to take a risk. He steered the whale-boat towards the shore. He and M'Leay landed unarmed and walked towards the small group of blacks. This action drove

"He went up to one who seemed the chief, seized him by the throat and pushed him back from the bank."

away any fears that may have been in their minds, and not only their fears but those of the others. For presently crowds of both parties were swimming over the river.

Sturt picked out their rescuer and made him a suitable present and by signs expressed his thanks. Then once more the boats were put out into the stream.

It was only then that the explorers were able to see how dangerous their position had been, for they counted over six hundred blacks massed on the banks.

From hostility they quickly passed to friendliness, and for some distance they kept with the boats. A few accompanied them for several days, and it was during that time that Sturt was able to learn something of their habits. They had, for instance, a wonderful skill in spearing fish. A black would slip feet first into the river, spear in hand, and without making a splash disappear under water. The next minute he would be up again with a fish neatly speared through the head.

That was the last time during the journey that the explorers ran any danger from natives, but other risks followed.

The Murray, as Sturt named the main river, became wider and the scenery more interesting. Then the river took a sudden bend to the south, and almost at once the voyage became rough. A strong southwest gale blew and so stormy was the river that progress became slow. It even became necessary to wait in camp at times before the waters were calm enough for launching the boats.

New tribes of blacks were met, but they were cleaner

and altogether more attractive than those of the interior. They proved friendly and helpful. Like the others they were interested in the clothes and equipment of the expedition, and nothing pleased the men more than to be allowed to wear a pair of trousers and swank in front of their women folk!

After thirty-three days of voyaging since they left their base on the Murrumbidgee, the explorers at last came to the lake through which the Murray makes its way to the sea. For the first time white men had explored one of the great rivers of the world.

Six years later the city of Adelaide was founded and the State of South Australia constituted. The district which lies to the west of the River Murray rightly bears the name of STURT, its discoverer.

II

Down the Colorado

THE Colorado is one of the most remarkable rivers in the world; it flows into the Gulf of California after cutting a passage for itself through the rocks; in places the walls of rock are from 4000 to 7000 feet high, rising sheer from the river as it boils down the trench or canyon.

The Indians had a legend about the origin of the river. Long ago a great and wise chief was stricken with grief at the death of his wife. One of the gods came to him and told him not to mourn as she was in a happier land. But this gave little comfort to the chief, so the god offered to take him to that happier land if, on his return, he would cease to grieve over his loss. The chief agreed, and they set off. The trail the god made is the Colorado, and on their return the god stamped the trail deep and filled it with a raging river so that no man would venture to follow it.

In 1869 J. W. Powell decided that he would like to take boats down through the series of canyons and so find out more about this extraordinary river. Many warned him not to attempt such a reckless feat, but he found nine men, including his brother, who were willing to take the risk. He himself had lost an arm in the American Civil War, but this handicap in no way worried him or them, though on one occasion, as will be related later, it nearly cost him his life.

He paid a preliminary visit to the region and made enquiries of Indians to see if they could give him any useful information, but they all warned him to beware of a river which was so obviously guarded by powerful spirits. One old chief told of how one of his tribe had tried to run one of the lesser canyons.

"The rocks," he said, holding his hands above his head, his arms vertical, and looking between them to the heavens, "the rocks h-e-a-p, h-e-a-p high; the water go h-oo-wwogh, h-oo-woogh; water-pony (boat) h-e-a-p buck; water catch 'em; no see 'em Injun any more! No see 'em squaw any more! No see 'em pappoose (child) any more!"

It was on 24 May 1869 that the party started from Green River City. They had four boats; three were of oak and twenty feet each in length; each was divided into three compartments, the fore and aft ones being covered in, partly to protect stores and partly to add to buoyancy. The fourth was a smaller boat of lighter build intended for speed.

They had practically no information to go upon, so their journey was a real piece of exploration, attended with unusual danger from falls, rapids and whirlpools.

Their method of procedure was as follows. Powell went ahead in his boat so that he could signal to the others what to do. When he approached a rapid, or fall, the oarsmen would backwater so that they would drift with the current as slowly as possible, though that 'slowly' would seem fairly quick to most people. If the leader could see a clear passage, or chute, he would go ahead and the others would follow. If however, as frequently happened, he found the channel blocked with rocks, they would pull to land. They would then lower the boats over the fall by ropes if that was possible; if not, they would have to portage (or carry) everything over the rocks until smoother water was reached. There was seldom any beach at such places, and portaging was hard work, as it meant many journeys clambering over boulders, carrying the boats as well as their gear and provisions.

Several times oars got broken on hidden rocks; then they had to fashion new ones out of driftwood. More serious accidents also happened. Here is an account of one which almost ended disastrously.

"During the afternoon (9 June) we came to a place where it was necessary to make a portage. The little boat was landed, and the others signalled to come up. When these rapids or broken falls occur, usually the channel is suddenly narrowed by rocks which have been tumbled from the cliffs or have been washed in. Immediately above the narrow, rocky channel, on one or both sides, there is often a bay of quiet water, in which we can land with ease. Sometimes the water descends with a smooth, unruffled surface, from the broad, quiet spread above, into the narrow, angry channel below. Great care must be taken not to pass over the brink of this deceptive pit.

"I walked along the bank to examine the ground, leaving one of my men with a flag to guide the other boats to the landing-place. I soon saw one of the boats make shore all right and felt no more concern; but a minute after, I heard a shout, and looking round saw one of the boats shooting down the centre. I felt that it was bound to go over, so I ran to save the third boat. A minute more, and she turned the point and headed for the shore. Then I turned down stream again, and scrambled along to look for the boat that had gone over. The first fall was not great, only ten or twelve feet, and we often ran such; but below, the river tumbled down again for forty or fifty feet, in a channel filled with dangerous rocks that broke the waves into whirlpools and beat them into foam. I passed round a great crag just in time to see the boat strike a rock, and, rebounding from the shock, careen and fill the open compartment with water. Two of the men lost their oars; she swung round, and was carried down at a rapid rate, broadside on, for a few yards, and struck amidships on another rock with great force, was broken quite in two, and the men were thrown into the river; the larger part of the boat floated up, and they soon seized it, and down the river they drifted, past rocks for a few hundred yards to a second rapid, filled with huge boulders, where the boat struck again, and was dashed to pieces, and the men and the fragments were soon carried beyond my sight. Running along, I turned a bend and saw a man's head above the water, washed about in a whirlpool below a great rock.

"It was Frank Goodman, clinging to the rock with a grip upon which life depended. I saw Howland trying to go to his aid from an island on which he had been washed. Soon he came near enough to reach Frank with a pole, which he extended towards him. The latter let go the rock, grasped the pole, and was pulled ashore. A third man was washed farther down the island, and was caught by some rocks and though somewhat bruised managed to get ashore in safety.

"And now the three men were on an island, with a swift, dangerous river on either side, and a fall below. The second boat was soon brought down, and Sumner, starting above as far as possible, pushed out. Right skilfully he plied the oars, and a few strokes set him on the island at the proper point. Then they all pulled the boat up stream, as far as they were able, until they stood in water up to their necks. One sat on a rock, and held the boat until the others were ready to pull, then gave the boat a push, clung to it with his hands, and climbed in as they pulled for mainland, which they reached in safety. We were as glad to shake hands with them as though they had been on a voyage round the world."

That was the only time they lost a boat, but few days passed without some exciting moments when one or other of them got a thorough soaking. The most serious aspect of the loss of the boat was that it contained provisions and some of their instruments. The Colorado runs through a desolate region where it is not easy to get food for the pot; they did some hunting when there seemed a chance of killing a sheep, but this always meant difficult climbing up the walls of the canyons.

It was just before they left the Green River and were approaching the Orange cliffs of the Colorado itself that Powell nearly lost his life in climbing the wall of the canyon. You will remember that he had only one arm, so climbing was not an easy business.

He and Bradley set off to get to the top of the wall of rock to get a general view of what might lie ahead. At

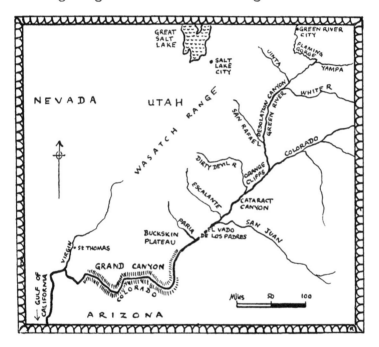

this point the sides of the canyon were like gigantic steps; once on a step it was easy going, but the climb from step to step was difficult. They had got to a height of some 700 feet, when they came to a face which was almost precipitous. Powell was ahead and he found a crevice which looked promising and he nearly reached the top before being stopped by a jutting rock. By making a spring he got a foothold and grasped an angle of rock just above his head. Then he found that he was not able to get higher or go back. If he let go with his one hand he would fall some eighty feet and probably finish by being dashed down into the river. He shouted to Bradley, who had found another way up and was now on the top. They were just out of reach of each other. There was no tree or bush to help. Powell was standing on his toes and straining to retain his grip. At last Bradley thought of a way; he took off his trousers and lowered them down; they were long enough to reach Powell, who still had to do some difficult manœuvring to grasp the unusual safety line. He hugged the rock as closely as he could, and then quickly let go with his hand and grasped the trousers. He was soon on top, but it had been a narrow escape.

They came across Indians at times who led a very hard life, but seemed contented in their primitive surroundings; at long intervals they would come to a trail leading across at a practicable point. Just before the Grand Canyon itself they found an old trail called El Vado de los Padres, after a priest who in 1776 had found that way when he was making a missionary journey to the north-west.

One interesting feature of their journey was the varying nature of the rocks; at times they would be floating between walls of marble, at others with granite rising all round them, and sometimes the canyon would be of lava.

It was on 13 August that they at last entered the

"*He hugged the rock as closely as he could, and then quickly let go with his hand and grasped the trousers.*"

Grand Canyon itself; they knew that what they had experienced so far was child's play compared with what the most famous canyon of all might have in store. Beaches were fewer, so they had to shoot the rapids, and these were more frequent than before. They had many a narrow escape from disaster. The dangers of the place got on the nerves of three of the men and they decided that they would go no farther; they believed that nothing but death awaited them, and tried hard to persuade Powell to abandon the expedition. They would rather, they said, run the risks of having to climb out of the canyon and search for some settlement, than get into the boats again. But Powell was determined to finish the exploration of the Grand Canyon; so they parted.

It was not long after the three had left that their gloomy forebodings were all but fulfilled. This is what happened.

They came to a series of falls where the river was too wild for shooting the rapids, so, in their usual manner, they landed on a shelf of rock and Powell went ahead to see if they could let the boats down by ropes. He discovered that it was too dangerous with whirlpools and rocks. But when he came back to warn them, he found that they had already got one boat on the line. Bradley was in the boat to fend it off the rocks and prevent the rope from fouling. But the current had already got the boat in its grip, and the men were finding it difficult to hold the rope, so they tied it round a rock and were going off to fetch an extra one. The river was at one minute dragging the boat to the full extent of the rope, and at the next dashing it against the rocks. It could not last long with such violent battering. Bradley saw his danger, and decided to take what he felt was the lesser risk of shooting the falls. The noise of the waters was too great for Powell to give him any advice.

Bradley took out his knife and cut the rope. Immediately the boat, with him in it, was swept down the river. The helpless spectators looked on in horror. They saw the boat engulfed in a great wave, and then come up again, only to be once more lost in the foam of the swirling waters. It seemed impossible for boat or man to live through such conditions. Then after what seemed hours of anxiety, but what was only a few seconds, they saw the boat emerge far down stream, and then to their amazement Bradley stood up and waved his hat!

As the days passed, their general condition became worse. They had lost valuable supplies in small accidents, and their stock of food was now very low. On 17 August Powell made this entry in his report.

"We have had rain, from time to time, all day, and have been thoroughly drenched and chilled; but between showers the sun shines with great power, so that we have rapid changes of temperatures, which are most disagreeable. It is especially cold in the rain to-night. The little canvas we have is rotten and useless; the rubber ponchos, with which we started from Green River City, have all been lost; more than half the party is without hats, and not one of us has an entire suit of clothes, and we have not a blanket apiece. So we gather drift wood, and build a fire; but after supper the rain, coming down in torrents, extinguishes it, and we sit up all night, on the rocks, shivering, and are more exhausted by the night's discomfort than by the day's toil."

The note for the following day reads: "The day is employed in making portages, and we advance but two miles on our journey. Still it rains."

From these extracts you can get some idea of the trials they had to endure in addition to the dangers of their journey.

At midday on 29 August they at last got out of the Grand Canyon after sixteen days of peril in its gloomy depths. They were at once struck by the calmness and comparative silence of the river and country into which they passed. All through the Canyon there had been the roar of the waters making it difficult even to talk with each other in any comfort.

That night they had a wonderful camp in peacefulness with the knowledge that they had achieved what they had set out to do in the face of strong opposition.

All the next day they steadily floated down the river towards the Rio Virgin. Suddenly one of the men shouted, 'There's an Indian, and three white men.' They came up to them at the mouth of the tributary. This party of three white men and an Indian had been sent down from Salt Lake City with instructions 'to watch for any fragments or relics that might drift down the stream'—so certain had people been that the expedition could only end in disaster!

The Indian was sent off to St. Thomas, a town about twenty miles up the Rio Virgin, with a message asking for supplies. He returned the next day with the news that a wagon load of food was on its way.

Not content with having defeated fate in 1869, one-armed Powell set out the following year to explore several of the rivers flowing into the Colorado, and to find out more about the various small Indian settlements in the region. He had an equally successful trip but without the dangers of his voyage down the Grand Canyon.

III

Amongst the Masai

In the days when the native still dominated Africa, the Masai were the fiercest and most dreaded of all the tribes. They occupied the land which we now call Kenya, after its highest mountain.

From boyhood the training was for war. The young men lived in warrior kraals and were fed on a diet of milk and meat. They did no menial work, that being left to the women. For weapons they had a spear with a blade two and a half feet long, a sword and a knob-kerry or club. The shield was of buffalo hide, oval in shape and decorated with striking designs.

The warrior was a terrifying figure as he set out for war. The most noticeable feature was a head-dress of ostrich feathers, with a cape of kite's feathers. All kinds of barbaric ornaments were worn on legs and arms. If you imagine a figure over six feet in height you can understand the terror the Masai spread throughout their part of Africa.

It was amongst these fierce warriors that Joseph Thomson proposed in 1883 to venture. His chief assets were an unfailing cheerfulness and considerable ingenuity in thinking out ways of impressing the native mind.

He took with him one white man, James Martin, an old sailor, and a party of natives as bearers. It had not been easy to persuade the blacks to join the ex-

"*The warrior was a terrifying figure as he set out for war.*"

pedition, for it meant travelling in the dreaded Masai country, but they trusted to the power of the white man to see them through.

They set out from Mombasa and took a north-westerly direction. Their first attempt failed and they were turned back, but Thomson was not easily defeated, and on his second march he was allowed to proceed.

As they came to the limits of each tribe's district it was necessary to get permission to go farther, and this meant long delays and much expenditure of gifts. Thomson soon discovered that unless he managed to impress the Masai warriors in some other way, his stock of beads, iron-wire and so on, would soon be finished. So he worked out a performance, as we may call it, to convince the natives that he was a great medicine-man with whom it would be unwise to interfere.

His main properties were a supply of Eno's fruit-salts, a galvanic battery for giving shocks, and his false teeth!

Here is an account of his usual 'turn', which had to be 'put on' whenever a fresh district was reached.

If possible they pitched their camp as secretly as they could and erected round it a fence or 'bomba' to prevent any sudden attack. Their presence could not long be hidden, and soon warriors would be pouring through the door in the fence to see what the strangers wanted.

For a time they would examine Thomson very carefully. They felt his hands and limbs, pulled at his clothes and generally mauled him about. This was always a trying business for him. But any sign of irritation would bring down a knobkerry on his head, so he suffered in silence.

When they had satisfied their curiosity he performed his first trick. He put his hand to his mouth and quickly removed his false teeth, showed them the gaps and then as quickly put the teeth back again. The effect on the Masai was usually astounding.

He went on to explain that such was his magic that he could remove any feature and replace it at will! Unfortunately on one occasion his bluff was called. One warrior seized him by the nose and tried to pull it off in the hope of seeing it replaced.

Next the galvanic battery was called into play. This would now be regarded as a very simple toy, but it was magic to the natives. After some persuasion one would be bold enough to take hold and the shock was sufficient to give him a new respect for Thomson as the guardian of this strange spirit.

Then would come the final trick. This is best described in Thomson's own words.

"I proceeded by laying out a small medicine-box with the lid open, showing all the array of phials, etc. Taking out my sextant, and putting on a pair of kid gloves (which impressed the natives enormously), I intently examined the contents. Discovering the proper *dawa* (charm), I prepared a mixture, and then getting ready some Eno's fruit-salt, I sang an incantation— generally something about 'Three blue-bottles'—over it. My voice not being astonishingly mellifluous, it did duty capitally for a wizard's. My preparations complete, and my servant being ready with a gun, I dropped the salt into the mixture; simultaneously the gun was fired, and, lo! up fizzed and sparkled the carbonic acid, causing the natives to shrink with intense dismay."

Amongst the Masai there is one curious custom. The way to bring good luck to anyone was to spit on him! Thomson, once his position as medicine-man was gained, had to spend quite a lot of time spitting on the natives as they queued up for the ceremony.

By these and other means he won his way through the lands of the fiercest tribes in Africa.

The most dangerous part of his journey was his trip to Mount Kenya. So familiar is that name to us that it is difficult to believe that one hundred years ago no white man had ever seen it, still less explored the surrounding country.

Thomson had followed the regular route taken by Arabs and others who were trading in ivory and slaves. That route is now followed by the line of the railway passing through Nairobi, the capital of Kenya. But when he proposed to turn off eastwards to the Mountain his native bearers begged him not to go. It meant entering districts quite unknown to the outside world, and they naturally feared the dangers. Along the trade route the Masai were used to bargaining with the Arabs and this prepared the way for any white man, but off that route anything might lie in wait.

He divided his party into two. The larger section was to go on the trade route under Martin's orders towards Lake Victoria Nyanza. The rest, about thirty strong, were to travel as light as possible with him towards Mount Kenya. It says much for his leader-

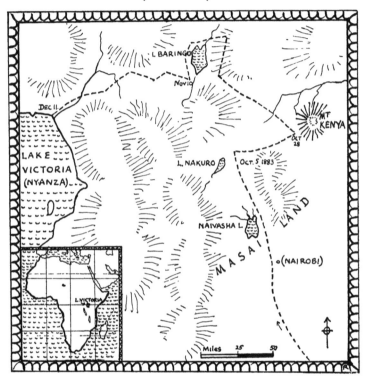

ship that he was able to persuade such a number to take the plunge into the unknown.

The map shows his route. He left the main party on 5 October. They went on along the route between the two ranges of mountains, while he turned off to the north-east.

They soon met with delays. Their first camp was pitched near a Masai kraal, and as quickly as possible they built a strong fence round the tents and shelters. Soon the young warriors came along to see the strangers. Then followed the usual performance of enquiry and magic.

The Masai were not at all willing for the party to go farther. They were suffering from a cattle plague and the beasts were dying in hundreds. Thomson was soon a bit sorry that he had established his position as a medicine-man, for they said, 'You are a great magician; you must stop with us and drive away the plague'.

Here was a problem! Once these fierce warriors learned that Thomson was no true magician, the knob-kerry would be his reward.

But he was not so easily daunted. For two days they kept him there while he puzzled over his difficulty. Then he saw a way out. He told them that his magic would not work till ten days after he had left. It took some time to get them to believe this, but at length, after much good-will spitting and Eno's, they let him go.

Time and time again they were held up. Thomson had estimated that they could get to the foot of Kenya in about eight days, but the district seemed full of warriors who all clamoured for presents and displays of magic. It was thus not until three weeks had passed that the explorer reached the base of the mountain.

By then his stock of presents was exhausted, and food supplies now depended on his skill as a hunter. It was impossible to spend more time in climbing the mountain, and it was dangerous to attempt to return by their outward route. The ten days in which his magic was to cure the cattle plague had long since passed, and with them, he suspected, his reputation as a medicine-man.

He had heard rumours of a large lake somewhere to the north-east of Mount Kenya, and he decided to go in that direction in the hope of discovering the exact position of the lake. This route would also have the advantage of getting them out of the Masai country, though there was always the possibility of running into a roving patrol.

They were now moving through trackless forest with innumerable streams; there was plenty of game to supply the place of their long-exhausted food supplies. Hunting for food was not always without risk, as the following incident illustrates.

One evening, while the men were pitching camp and making the fence, Thomson set off with his headman, Brahim, in search for food. They had not gone far before they sighted a buffalo on the edge of a forest clearing. They stalked him until they were within forty yards, when Thomson fired and hit him in the hip. The animal lumbered off into the forest. He was obviously badly wounded and could not get far, but a buffalo is a dangerous beast when roused; to follow him into the bush was a risky business but meat was needed and the risk had to be taken.

The two men skirted the forest until they found an opening in the dense undergrowth. They had to crawl along what was little better than a tunnel without being able to see more than six feet ahead. They paused and listened, but could hear nothing. Slowly they wormed their way forward until Brahim stopped his master and silently pointed towards a thicker part of the undergrowth.

Thomson fired again, dropped his gun and bolted for the open as quickly as possible. This does not sound very dignified, but he was not worried about style! He was out for necessary food, and had no intention of trying to stop a buffalo in a narrow tunnel.

It was as well he did, for the beast was at his heels, but it stopped at the edge of the forest and once more charged off in another direction, this time making for the heart of the bush.

Retrieving his gun, Thomson followed. Not a sound betrayed the two trackers. A sign with the finger or a look would indicate a drop of blood or fresh tracks. The first part was fairly easy going as it was more open, but after two hours' tracking they came to dense forest again. The freshness of the blood showed that they were close on their victim.

Once more they had to creep forward on all fours. Brahim was at the time leading, when suddenly he stiffened with one ear forward listening. Then slowly he crept back and his master took his place. What next happened is best told in Thomson's own words.

"Inch by inch I ventured forward, keeping myself as ready as my cramped position would admit. I tried to pierce the gloom, and listened for some sound. Suddenly I became petrified as a sound, like a sigh of pain, reached my ears. I held my breath as I strained to locate where it came from. I was certainly within a few feet of that most dreaded of all animals, but whether it was right in front or standing alongside of me, I was quite unable to make out.

"What was I to do? I dared not move. I was fixed. I cast a glance back at my companion, and we smiled in a sickly manner. Something had to be done! At last, therefore, I pushed aside a small branch. The next moment there was a grunt and a crashing of bushes, as the buffalo sprang to his feet. Thinking that he meant to charge, I threw myself back into the heart of a bush to avoid the rush if possible. The crashing of the bushes in the contrary direction, however, relieved us of further fears, and soon we were mopping our faces and generally recovering tone."

Once more they took up the trail. Thomson managed to fire twice and at length brought him down. It was a hard-earned meal for all the party.

They made good progress for some days, and then at last Thomson received the only reward an explorer really enjoys: he discovered Lake Baringo, many times heard of by rumour but never seen by white man up to that time.

It lay at the bottom of a great rift and the party first saw it from the top of the precipitous walls of rock which bounded it on two sides. The descent was difficult and Thomson went on with Brahim and another man to find a better way down. They at length came across a faint track evidently used by animals. Thomson took this track and told the two others to wait for the rest of the party.

It took him much longer than he expected to reach the bottom. He looked up and his men gave a signal which he thought meant that they had found a better path, so he went on in the hope of picking it up farther on. But no sign of any other path could be seen.

He shouted, but there was no reply. He turned back and at intervals shouted to attract his men's attention. Just as he was making up his mind to find a tree in which to spend the night, a gun was fired off, and by shouting and gun-fire he was able to rejoin his two companions. The rest of the party was nowhere to be seen. They fired their guns but there was no answer.

It was now getting dark and their position was dangerous. The place was alive with buffaloes and rhinoceroses. They at length found a stream running down towards the lake; this they followed. To add to their difficulties rain came down in torrents. They decided to get a fire going and spend the night as best they could. The following account of fire-lighting under difficulties is worth giving in full.

"By a good deal of groping about we contrived to gather some firewood together, but then to our dismay we had *only three matches* and these bad, while we could find nothing but damp grass. Before venturing to strike we held a consultation as to who was the best at striking a light. Brahim was chosen. The scene was very strange as we gathered round him in breathless interest, in the almost pitch darkness of the night, with great trees overhead, and dense bush around haunted by wild beasts. The first match was struck, there was a faint flicker, and then darkness. With an imprecation Brahim threw it savagely aside, and we all indulged in expletives, each 'after his kind'. The second attempt was watched with further excitement, but it went out like the other. The last match was taken in hand. To our unspeakable relief it caught. Nursing it as if it were divine fire, I kept leaves of my note-books burning till some twigs ignited.

"In a short time we were drying ourselves before a glorious fire. We were quite prepared to think our situation a piece of rather good fun, as we each munched about a mouthful of Indian corn. The rain fortunately stopped, and, setting a watch, we were able to enjoy a snatch of sleep, only broken at intervals by the movements of some buffalo or rhinoceros whose nightly rambles had been disturbed by our blazing fire."

The next morning they went on down the stream; they had some hard going that day but towards evening they rejoined their main party under Martin and found all well and hearty. There was, however, no sign of the other Kenya men, and it was two days before they turned up. They had lost touch and had wandered about trying to find a way down to the lake.

After a rest in the camp, the whole party set off for Lake Victoria Nyanza, and there we will leave them. Their adventures were by no means over, but they had blazed the trail which in later years was to open up the country we now call KENYA.

IV

A Herring-boat in the North-West Passage

IN 1576 Martin Frobisher left the Thames with two small ships of 20 tons each to find a way into the Pacific round the north of America. This was the first attempt to discover a North-West Passage. To us it may seem an absurd idea, but in those days men argued that there must be a shorter way into the Pacific than by sailing the 10,000 miles south to Cape Horn.

For more than three hundred years the search went on, and many famous names are connected with it. If you look at a map of that region you will see the record of the men who risked all for this idea: Frobisher Bay, Hudson Bay, Davis Strait, Baffin Bay, Franklin Strait, McClintock Channel, and finally Amundsen Gulf.

It was Roald Amundsen who conquered the Passage in his 47 ton herring-boat in the years 1903 to 1907. Long before that date it had been realised that even if such a Passage existed it would be useless for shipping on account of the narrow channels, and of the severe ice conditions. But men do not like giving up unsolved problems, and in the same way in which they obstinately and gloriously try to climb Mount Everest, so they went on searching for the North-West Passage.

The young Norwegian was drawn to the adventure chiefly for the fun of the thing, but people were beginning to ask, 'What is the use of these expeditions?' just as they ask nowadays, 'What is the use of climbing Everest?'

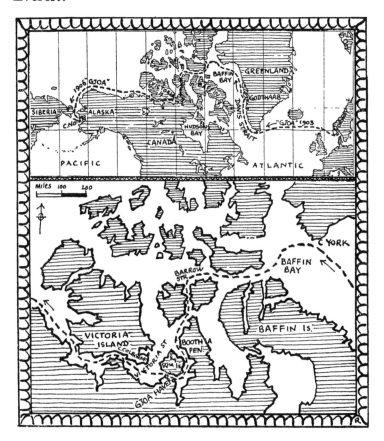

The answer is that such expeditions are not half as useful as a piece of soap, but much more exciting, and they challenge men to put out all their energy and skill, and they demand great courage and physical endurance.

Perhaps it was in answer to such questions that Amundsen tacked on to his plans a scientific purpose; he would take observations and record readings in order to determine the position of the Magnetic North Pole. This is not the same as the Geographical North Pole, but is the area to which the compass needle points.

On 16 June 1903 he set sail with six companions from Oslo in the *Gjoa*, a herring-boat which had been built in 1872. A 13 H.P. motor was put in, and other changes were made for her new employment.

Amundsen expected to be away for five years. During the winter months they would be frozen in, and they might expect all kinds of delays and difficulties in getting free each summer. That is why he stocked the ship for such a long period.

Stores for five years for six men take up a lot of room, and it was only by the most ingenious packing that all was safely crammed into the little vessel. In addition to six men, there were six dogs to be accommodated and fed.

They set their course for Greenland, and there put in at the settlement of Godthaab on the west coast. It was there that Nansen had arrived fifteen years before after making the first ski-crossing of Greenland.

They now took on board some more equipment, such as sledges, kayaks and skis, as well as twenty barrels of petroleum. It was not easy to get this extra cargo in the ship, but at length all was ready for the next stage of the adventure.

Their plan was to sail as far north as ice conditions would allow, and then to turn westwards. Baffin Bay was fairly open, so they were able to get as far as Cape York. Fog proved more dangerous than ice. In the Arctic the fogs are denser than in any other part of the world, and when the ice is about any ship runs considerable danger.

However, they were fortunate in getting a clear passage, and after sailing through Barrow Strait, they turned southwards through Franklin Strait. The Magnetic North Pole made its presence felt by the erratic behaviour of the compass.

At this time the expedition nearly came to a sudden and tragic end. Amundsen was sitting in his cabin one evening when he was startled by the dread cry of 'Fire! Fire!' No more terrible cry could be heard on a wooden vessel far from civilisation. He rushed out to find flames leaping out of the engine-room skylight.

All hands soon got to work. They knew the danger, for the fire was close to their drums of petroleum, and once those got heated they would explode and the expedition would be over. One man rushed down into the engine room to help the engineer, who had stuck to his post in spite of the risk. The others pumped water on to the fire for very life. Soon they had it under control.

Later they discovered the cause. The fire had broken out in some cleaning waste which was soaked in petroleum. But it was more interesting to discover that but for the prompt obedience to orders the ship would have been blown to bits.

The previous afternoon it had been reported to Amundsen that one of the petroleum tanks was leaking. He gave instructions for the remaining oil to be put into an empty tank. This order was at once carried out. When they cleared up the engine room after the fire, they found that the tap of the emptied tank had been wrenched right off during the fight with the fire. Had it not been emptied, over 100 gallons of petroleum would have spurted into the burning engine room.

They were now passing along a low-lying coast with islands here and there, and navigation became tricky. On 1 September they were between Boothia and King William Land, and as the weather became threatening and the wind rose, Amundsen decided to anchor for the night. The gale increased steadily, and heavy sleet fell.

Towards morning the wind lessened and veered round to the west. So anchor was weighed, and once more they began to feel their course very carefully. To leeward of them there was a low-lying island with banks running out to the east. It seemed all clear, then without warning they ran aground, but fortunately got off again almost at once.

Shortly afterwards they struck again, and from the crow's nest it was possible to see that they had grounded on a large submerged reef of some considerable extent.

A boat was launched and soundings taken. From these it appeared that the best way was aft, but they had already been aground on a bank in that direction. Soundings gave little hope of going forwards, but there was no possible alternative. The reef shallowed somewhat, but there was not much more than a fathom of water over it. Now the *Gjoa* was, as we have seen, overloaded, and drew just over ten feet. The chances of getting over the reef were therefore small.

They had to lighten the ship. Overboard went twenty-five cases of dog pemmican; these weighed about 4 cwt. each. Next they packed all the other cases on one side of the deck in the hope that this would make the ship heel over.

Unfortunately they had grounded at high tide, and so every hour gave them less water in which to move. At last they gave the task up until the next high tide, which would be about 7 that evening. Meantime the kedge was put over, and every preparation made to take full advantage of the tide. But all proved in vain. High tide came and went and they were still stuck fast. Patiently they waited for the morning.

At 2 a.m. the next day it was blowing fresh from the north. Then the ship began to move as if it were being shaken. The wind increased and soon a gale was blowing hard, with sleet and hail. They hove on the kedge again and again but with no result. The little ship was pitching violently.

What was to be done? They decided to try to get her off with the sails—a desperate measure under such conditions. With the spray flying over the decks, and the wind howling round them in great gusts, they struggled to get the sails set. Then began what Amundsen called "a method of sailing not one of us is ever likely to forget".

"The mighty press of sail," he wrote, "and the

high choppy sea combined, had the effect of lifting the vessel up and pitching her forward again among the rocks, so that we expected every moment to see her planks scattered in the sea. The false keel was splintered, and floated up. All we could do was to watch the course of events and calmly await the issue."

It needs a good deal of self-control to wait calmly under such conditions, for it looked as though they were coming to the end.

Amundsen weighed up the possibilities; he must either abandon the *Gjoa*, take to the boats and let her be smashed, or, he must dare all and remain on board with the real possibility of losing all hands.

He decided on the first course, and gave orders for the boats to be cleared and loaded. But one of his men, Lund, came forward with another suggestion. Why not jettison all the rest of the deck cargo? That might lighten the ship enough to get her free.

It was a desperate idea, but they were in a desperate position. It was received with cheers by the crew, and Amundsen agreed that it was worth trying.

So overboard as fast as possible they threw all the cases of goods which remained on deck. Then Amundsen climbed into the rigging to see what the new position was like.

The ship was being forced to the end of the reef which stood out above water, and presently the little vessel was lifted high, and then flung down with terrific force on to the bare rock.

Everything depended now on their finding a way out through the shoals round the reef.

"So overboard as fast as possible they threw all the cases of goods which remained on deck."

Hansen, the second in command, was at the wheel. Presently he cried out, 'There's something wrong with the rudder! It won't steer!'

This meant the end, but no sooner had they realised that a rudderless ship would be out of all control, than Hansen shouted out, 'The rudder is all right again!'

A miracle had happened. The first shock had lifted the rudder so that it was held with the pins on the mountings: the last shock had shaken it back into place. No wonder the whole crew cheered at such an amazing chance.

But at last they were free from that horrible reef. As soon as they were once more in deep water, they dropped both anchors, and got some long-needed rest. They were wet through and through and were almost frozen.

The region they were in was uncharted except very roughly, and great care had to be taken in navigation. For the rest of the time one man was always in the crow's nest, and another was using the lead.

Winter was drawing near, and they had to look for a safe place in which the ship would be frozen up for the dark months. They discovered an ideal harbour to the south-east of King William Land, and there they berthed and made preparations for their winter quarters. They called their bay Gjoa Haven.

On 14 September they began to unload the ship. The dogs were first taken ashore. Then an aerial rope-way was rigged and the packing cases brought up from the hold and landed. These cases were specially made for the purpose. An outer case protected an inner one. On shore they took off the outer cases and used these for building the walls of their special huts; they had a store hut, an observatory, and a magnetic hut.

By the beginning of October the ice was already thick enough for them to walk ashore. When all was ship-shape, they got to work on their various jobs. Some had charge of the scientific observations, others were hunters and went off after reindeer and other game. One important arrangement was the 'Fire Station'. This consisted of a hole in the ice with a snow hut built over it. Throughout the winter the hole was kept open so that there should be a good supply of water in case of fire. Luckily it was never wanted.

Here it is not necessary to give an account of their winter activities in any detail. They made friends with a band of Eskimo; they kept careful scientific readings with their instruments, and studied the nature of the surrounding country as far as possible.

One valuable thing they learned from the Eskimo was the correct way of making a snow-hut or igloo. On their sledge expeditions later on they built snow-huts instead of using tents as they found them much more comfortable under Arctic conditions.

An old Eskimo named Teraiu was their instructor. First they had to know how to recognise snow of the right quality. Then with special knives they cut out large blocks, and built up walls, and finally the roof. As soon as the structure was finished, the inside had to be heated so that all would become one solid mass.

With practice they found that they could build a hut for four men in about an hour and a half. Amundsen found that the gain in warmth and comfort was well worth the extra time taken in making a hut instead of pitching a tent.

In the spring of 1904 they had a sledge expedition to locate the Magnetic North Pole, and during that summer they explored the coast and surveyed it carefully. Another winter was passed as the first in studying the Eskimo, and in making their long series of scientific observations.

It is interesting to record Amundsen's opinion of the strange people who inhabit those Arctic wastes. "The Eskimo, living absolutely isolated from civilisation of any kind, are undoubtedly the happiest, healthiest, most honourable, and most contented of people. My sincerest wish is that civilisation may *never* reach them."

At last the summer of 1905 came, and the time for setting sail once more for the search for the North-West Passage. On 13 August 1905 the *Gjoa* was free, and set sail. They had to take the precaution of sounding for a channel; they were hampered by fog, and also by the fact that the compass would not work in that area; it was too close to the Magnetic Pole.

During their surveying expeditions of the previous summer they had been able to gather a certain amount of information about possible courses which the ship might follow. One thing they were certain of was that the channels were all narrow and full of dangerous reefs and rocks. A larger vessel would have been useless. It might be said that they felt their way foot by foot.

Here is Amundsen's account of one of the difficult parts. "Sharp stones faced us on every side, low-lying rocks of all shapes, and we bungled through as if we were drunk. The lead flew up and down, down and up, and the man at the helm had to pay very close attention and keep his eye on the look-out man, who jumped about in the crow's nest like a maniac, throwing his arms about for starboard and port respectively, keeping on the move all the time to watch the track. The anchors were clear to drop, should the water be too shallow. We barely managed to scrape over. In the afternoon things got worse than ever; it was just like sailing through an uncleared field."

So for days they crept along. They got into Victoria Strait, which was full of ice-floes, but not dangerous enough to stop the ship. And on 17 August they anchored on the west side of Cape Colborne. They had solved the mystery of the North-West Passage, and were through into known waters.

On 26 August they sighted their first ship, the American *Charles Hanson*. They went aboard and exchanged news with the Captain, and on their return they brought as a present from him a sack of potatoes and another of onions; both luxuries after two years in the Arctic.

The rest of that voyage does not concern us here. They had set out to achieve the dream of centuries, and had accomplished their aim.

They finished at Cape Nome on the western coast of

Alaska, and there they were given the heartiest welcome that Americans can give.

In after years Amundsen carried out many other feats of exploration. He sailed through the North-East Passage, he discovered the South Pole, and he was the first to fly over the North Pole in the airship *Norge*. In 1928 he set off over the Arctic by aeroplane to rescue the Italian flyer Nobile; but since he left Norway, no word has been heard of him: a not unfitting end for a great explorer.

V

Robbed by Arabs

IN 1840 a young man of twenty-three, Henry Layard, set out from Jerusalem to visit the ruins of the ancient city of Petra on the edge of the Arabian Desert. The site had been discovered in 1814 by the German traveller, Burckhardt, but there was still much to be learned; Layard was perhaps as much attracted by the risks of the journey as by curiosity, for there were considerable dangers from the wandering tribes of Arabs who owned no one as master or overlord. Even to-day travel in those parts is not to be lightly undertaken.

One piece of sound advice he was given before setting out. "You must travel", he was told, "either as an important personage with many servants and an armed escort, or alone, as a poor man with nothing to excite the cupidity of the tribes." The choice was not difficult, for Layard could not afford to be a 'personage' even if he had wished it.

He therefore left Jerusalem in January 1840 with an Arab boy, Antonio, as his servant and interpreter. Their equipment consisted of a small tent, a supply of rice and flour, a carpet for sitting and sleeping, a compass, some medicines (for all Arabs think an Englishman is a doctor, a *hakim*), and a double-barrelled gun. In his saddle-bags he had a change of linen, maps and his note-books. Two mules carried the gear.

They took the road south to Hebron.

Palestine was at that period under the government of Egypt, so Layard had taken the precaution of getting some letters of introduction to Egyptian officials and also to some of the sheiks. The English Consul had given him similar help but said that he could take no responsibility. "If you escape being murdered," he said, "you will in all probability be robbed of everything you possess." The second part of this forecast proved the true one.

At Hebron, therefore, Layard got into touch with the officials; he wanted them to put him under the protection of some Arab sheik going south, and he also needed to get camels in place of his mules.

This was arranged, and after much haggling over costs, Sheik Defallah undertook to supply two camels, but he said that he could not guarantee the traveller's safety as the Arab tribes in the area were at war with each other.

The next morning they set off, and Layard had his first experience of camel riding. "Once, when descending a steep hill, my beast took a fancy to start off in a kind of awkward gallop. I tried to check it with the halter which was fastened to its nose, but it only turned its head round as I pulled with all my might, and looked me full in the face, without stopping or even slackening its speed. I clung to the pack-saddle. My saddle-bags fell off first, my carpet followed, and, losing my balance, I slipped over the tail of the animal and came full length to the ground."

Towards evening they came to the sheik's camp in one of the many valleys running down to the Dead

*My saddle-bags fell off first, my carpet followed, and, losing my balance,
slipped over the tail of the animal and came full length to the ground."*

Sea. Here Layard was hospitably treated. The Arabs have a high standard of hospitality; once anyone has become their guest by sharing in a meal, he is safe from all danger, and Layard found it a good plan to make friends in this way as quickly as possible. At first he found their customs rather difficult for an Englishman. Here for instance is how a meal was served.

"A great mess of rice and boiled mutton was brought to the tent about two hours after my arrival. The sheik's brother and his friends ate with me, dipping their fingers into the large wooden bowl and picking out the savoury bits, which they presented to me."

He was suffering from toothache, so one Arab offered to remove the tooth. The dentistry was decidedly rough. "His instruments consisted of a short knife or razor, and a kind of iron awl. He bade me sit on the ground, and then took my head firmly between his knees. After cutting away the gums, he applied the awl to the roots of the tooth, and, striking the other end of it with all his might, expected to see the tooth fly into the air. But it was a double one and not to be removed by such means. He insisted upon a second trial. But the only result was that he broke off a large piece of the tooth, and I had suffered sufficient agony to decline a third experiment."

The next morning he set off again, now accompanied by two of the tribesmen, Musa and Awad, both armed with long guns. Their route was through the wildest of country, and both the tribesmen and Antonio were terrified of attacks from other Arabs.

They insisted on absolute silence, and, selecting a secluded gully for the night's camp, they took turns at watching for any enemy.

They set off again next morning at 2 o'clock as there was clear moonlight. Musa went ahead as a scout, and came galloping back later with the news that he had seen strange horsemen in the distance. Presently three Bedouins on horseback, carrying long tufted spears, approached from three sides with hostile intentions. Musa and Awad prepared for defence, and Layard also got ready for action with his gun. The sight of the guns made the horsemen halt. They declared that they were friendly, and only wanted bread. They dismounted and handed their spears to Awad as a sign of their good intentions. Then they parleyed. Afterwards Antonio told his master that the Bedouins had suggested to the two guards that they should join together to kill and rob 'the Frank' as they called Layard, but Musa and Awad, mindful of the strict law of hospitality, refused. So the Bedouins rode off.

To throw them off the track the party now followed a devious route among the low hills, as the Arabs were convinced that the three horsemen had not given up their evil intentions. But no further trouble came from them.

Another day's journey brought them to Petra. Here Layard prepared to make a thorough examination of the ruins, to copy the inscriptions on the tombs and monuments, and to make sketches. But no sooner had he started on his work than a hoard of Arabs came out of the ruined buildings and surrounded him.

"They were known", wrote Layard, "to be treacherous and bloodthirsty, and a traveller had rarely, if ever, ventured among them without the protection of some powerful chief or without a guard."

The leader of this band demanded a large sum of money which he said was due from all travellers. On Layard's firm refusal, the band advanced, but he raised his gun determined to sell his life dearly; at the same time he warned them that he was under the protection of the Egyptian Government. This made them pause and consult together. Layard then took a bold course; he walked off quietly to look at the ruins as if he was not interested in such ruffians. Such conduct surprised them. He spent the greater part of the day in examining the ruins, and he was no further molested though the gang kept watch over his every movement.

Layard felt that it would be wise to cut short his visit, as even he did not dare spend the night amongst such hostile men; so they camped in a valley on the way back, but they had little sleep for a watch was necessary.

They did not return to Jerusalem, but kept to the east of the Dead Sea, making for Kerak, where it had been arranged for Musa and Awad to return to their tribe with the camels. Layard had decided that he would make his way north to Damascus.

Their next adventure took place as they neared Kerak. At breakfast one day they were joined by a sheik with several men. Suddenly the sheik attacked Awad and tried to wrest the saddle-bags from him.

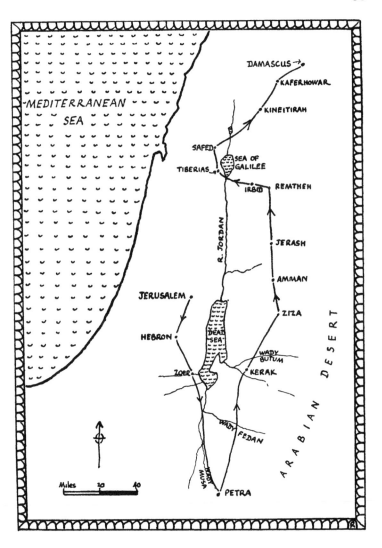

Layard seized him and demanded an explanation. The sheik said that he wanted a large sum of money for permission to pass through his tribal area, otherwise he would attack with his men. Layard acted promptly. He pointed his gun at the sheik, and ordered Antonio to disarm him. This was done; pistols, a knife, and a club being taken from him. Then Layard went on with his breakfast, but kept his gun handy, while the sheik sat in front of him. They continued the journey with the sheik walking in front as a kind of hostage. But when the rough road entered the next valley, they saw an encampment of Arabs on the hillside. These men rushed down at once on sight of the travellers. Layard gripped the sheik by the arm and held the muzzle of his gun close to his head. The sheik was terrified and cried out to his men, for this was his tribe, to do no harm. But already several had robbed the camels of their loads, and one man, more ferocious than the rest, rushed at Layard with raised spear. The sheik at length persuaded the man to give up his murderous intention. Meantime, Awad had shouted out that they had letters to the Governor of Kerak and were under the protection of the Egyptian Government. This too had a quieting effect; but Layard was taking no risks; he still gripped the sheik and pushed him onwards toward Kerak.

As they came out of the valley they saw ahead another Arab encampment, and Antonio recognised the tribe as under the Governor of Kerak. As soon as Layard was sure of this, he released the hostile sheik, who immediately scuttled away to his tribe.

At the camp Layard was received hospitably by the sheik, who said that his guest had had a lucky escape from one of the worst tribes in Arabia. They at once went on to Kerak; the Governor was absent, but his son, Ahmed, read the letter of introduction and, when he heard Layard's story, immediately ordered his men to get ready to recover the stolen goods.

The party set off. Ahmed entered the tent of the robber sheik, and after the proper ceremony of taking coffee, and smoking, he made a speech upraiding the robbers for attacking anyone under the protection of the Government, finishing with the words, 'This man walks with God, whilst you walk with the Devil!'

After a stormy discussion it was decided to return as much of the property as could be found, and gradually articles were collected first from one tent and then another. One pair of trousers had been ingeniously turned into a jacket! By the time most were got together, it was dusk, so Layard and Ahmed stopped the night in the robber camp.

When they returned to Kerak, Ahmed demanded a present; first a gun, then a cloak, then the carpet which Layard used as a bed. But the traveller refused as all these were necessary to him. In revenge Ahmed forbade his people to provide camels or horses, for by this time Awad and Musa had returned home with the other camels. At last Ahmed tired of his efforts, and promised to put Layard under the protection of Sheik Suleiman who would be passing through Kerak the next day on his way to Ammon; he also offered two mules at a price. Layard accepted.

The Sheik Suleiman seemed friendly and gladly offered his protection for the next stage of the journey. But it was not long before Layard found that he was the victim of a plot between the sheik and Ahmed. The following morning, as camp was being struck, the sheik explained that Layard must pay him thirty pounds, and said that he himself had paid this to Ahmed as he understood Layard was a rich man. This treachery infuriated Layard, who wanted to return to Kerak and confront Ahmed. He certainly did not lack courage under the most dangerous circumstances.

He explained to Suleiman that first of all he had no such sum of money on him, and second, if he had he would not part with it under such conditions. The sheik at length saw the force of the first argument, and said that he would see Ahmed later; there is no record of that meeting unfortunately. Then Suleiman changed his tone, and became quite friendly again. Layard noticed several times that if he was firm the Arabs would give way and seemed to harbour no grudge.

So Layard passed from sheik to sheik; usually with the same experience of demands for large sums of money, and then a more helpful attitude. At last he came within sight of the Sea of Galilee; he had decided to cross to Tiberias and travel by that town to Damascus, as the route to the east of the lake was too dangerous. Five miles from the lake his last guide suddenly announced that he could go no farther and, without more ado, unloaded Layard's gear, and set off with the mules. So there he was with Antonio, his gear, and no mules.

There was nothing for it but to carry what they could and set off on foot for Tiberias.

It was a weary trudge, and it was made worse by the worry of not knowing how they could manage to get to Damascus. But one piece of luck was theirs. As they entered the town they met an old man in European clothes who asked if he could help them. He was a Polish Jew who had retired to Palestine. Layard told him their adventures, and the old man invited them to his house. He further offered to lend his guest money to get to Damascus, as he said he knew he could trust an Englishman.

Antonio now decided to return to his home in Jerusalem; his master parted with him regretfully, for he had proved a faithful servant under all dangers.

Layard was able to hire a horse and guide as far as Safed, and there after some trouble he hired another man with two mules to take him to Damascus. The man was not too eager to go even for payment, as he said there were tribes of Bedouins roaming the wild country ready to attack any travellers. But at last he agreed to start.

It was pouring with rain and the roads were in a deplorable condition, so it was anything but a pleasant journey, but Layard was cheered by the prospect of ending his journey. He had still another trial to undergo.

After two days' travelling they reached the village of Kaferhowar, and here the muleteer flatly refused to go farther. He said that enemies of his would seize him if he went nearer Damascus. Layard tried in vain to hire more mules; finally he had to be content with a man who offered to guide him to Damascus, but could hire no beasts of burden. So Layard's gear was divided between them, and they set off on foot.

They were going by rough paths to avoid roads where robbers might be in wait, and it was not long before Layard's shoes gave out, and he became footsore as the weary miles passed.

Even when they were within sight of Damascus they were stopped by an Arab, who demanded where they were going. Layard showed his passport, but the man evidently did not read; the last small gold coin the traveller had solved this last obstacle.

"We lost no time", he wrote, "in going our way. My guide left the high road, diverged into by-lanes and climbed over the ruined walls of gardens. I almost ran until we were within the gates of the city. We passed through them with a crowd of peasants."

He went at once to the house of the British Consul, who "was not a little surprised at being addressed by an Englishman clad in scarcely more than a tattered cloak, almost shoeless, and bronzed and begrimed by long exposure to sun and weather and to the dirt of Arab tents".

Layard next entered Damascus in 1878 when he was British Ambassador to Turkey. He was then received by the Governor, and passed through welcoming crowds of people of all races and creeds. It was a strange contrast to the young man in a tattered cloak!

VI

Brilliant Failure

WE rightly honour men who are first in accomplishing some great feat, such as reaching the Poles, or flying across the Atlantic. But we must not forget that what they have done has only been possible because many have previously blazed a trail, or even lost their lives in finding out how to overcome great obstacles. The final success is always spectacular, but we must remember the parties which have gone time and time again to plan for the victory. We sometimes forget the names of the pioneers.

Here I want to tell you of an expedition which failed, in the sense that it did not achieve its purpose, but it showed the way to others, and in doing so did great work.

In Alaska, that frozen land of North America, is Mount McKinley. It is 20,309 feet high, and is the highest mountain north of Panama. There are at least eleven higher mountains in the world, but McKinley presents peculiar problems. First of all it is in the cold north; the only routes are over glaciers thirty miles in length. Then it rises very abruptly. Now in the Andes and Himalayas the route for many thousands of feet is by a series of plateaux, and the climbers can take the first approaches by stages. McKinley however presents some 17,000 feet of ice and snow every inch of which has to be climbed laboriously.

It will therefore be seen that the ascent of this mountain is a very difficult problem. Three expeditions, 1906, 1910 and 1912, solved the problem of the best way up. Two names must be mentioned—Belmore Browne, an artist, and Clifford Parker, a professor. They took part in all three expeditions, and came within a short distance of reaching the summit in 1912. The mountain was climbed in 1913 by Stuck and Karstens, but the credit for the previous 'trail breaking' must be given to Browne and Parker, and it is with their 1912 attempt that we are here concerned.

Their attempts in 1906 and 1910 were made from the south-east slopes. The approach looks simple; there is a river, the Chulitna, running close to the foot of the ridge. It must, however, be remembered that this is not a pleasant stream like the Thames but a turbulent river fed by glaciers, and frozen for part of the year.

Those attacks on the south-east face were unsuccessful. They found it impossible to get to the summit from that direction. Having failed there, the next problem was to find a more practicable route. They argued that if they could get on the other side of the range, there might well be a better way up on the north face. But how to get there?

Very little was known of the Alaska Range, and no one seemed to be certain whether there was a pass over or not. It was believed that prospectors had crossed, but where or how no one could tell.

Finally they decided to go up the Chulitna River route again as far as seemed useful and then search for a pass, cross, and then attack from the other side.

It would be necessary to take considerable supplies, as they would be out of touch with civilisation for some time. Here it may be interesting to say some-

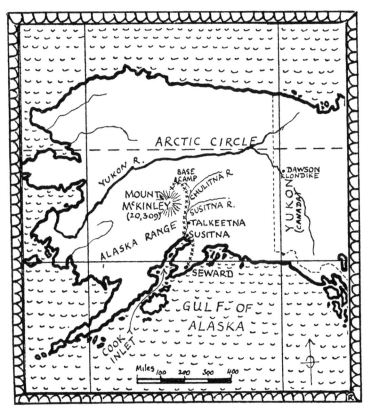

thing on the question of food. On the harder stretches of climbing when every ounce had to be back-packed, they relied on pemmican, hardtack, sugar, raisins and tea. Pemmican is a form of food introduced to explorers by the Red Indians. It consists of lean meat, dried in the sun, and pounded, mixed with fat to form a paste, and finally made into cakes. Hardtack explains itself—we should call it ship-biscuit. While they were able to use dogs and sledges they could of course have greater variety of food.

You have heard Americans called 'dough boys', and may have wondered where the name came from. It was originally used for men who had been in Alaska, because they lived partly on 'sour-dough'—and this formed a substantial part of our explorers' food. Try making some for yourself. A batter is made of plain flour and water; the pot is then hung up in a warmish place until the batter sours, that is, ferments. Sugar and salt and some soda (not baking powder) and more flour are stirred in, and then the thick dough is shaped into cakes and baked in front of a fire. Old-timers believed that the longer the dough was left to sour the better. One records that "our sour-dough pail has been going continuously for nine months now, and is getting better all the time. Do not be dismayed at the odour!"

As opportunity came they varied their supplies by hunting, and in this way added caribou meat to their diet, and also the white sheep of those parts.

On the outward journey they made caches (or dumps) of supplies for their return. This was another tip originally learnt from the Indians; to the Indian a cache is sacred even if he is in distress himself, for he knows that someone is depending on that food and gear when coming that way again.

This is the method of making a cache. A platform of logs is made large enough to take the stores. This is then hung from a tree, or trees, so that it is out of reach of animals. The most annoying of these wild beasts is the wolverine, and to protect a cache from his attentions, the bough of the tree is sheathed in tin from old petrol cans. The wolverine is a most powerful animal, and with its iron jaws and sharp claws it can open the strongest box; moreover, it not only takes food to eat, but just destroys everything it can get at.

Our explorers arrived at Seward by ship in the winter time. They had decided to do the overland trek at that period because there would be firm snow for sledging, and the going would therefore be easier. This would also give them plenty of time for reaching their final base camp before summer.

The first stage was to Susitna Station. At Seward they got into touch with a mail-carrier named Vause who was going to Susitna and knew the trail well. He led with a sledge carrying five hundred pounds of goods and mail, with six dogs.

The trail was not in good condition; the weather had been warm for the time of the year (February) and the sledges were often breaking through the soft crust; sudden drops in the level would sometimes mean the sledge turning over, and five hundred pounds weight takes some shifting!

The distance travelled each day depended on the condition of the trail, and on the way to Susitna it varied from fourteen to fifty-five miles. They took seventeen days over that first stage.

At Susitna they were joined by two other members of the party, Aten and La Voy, who had been employed chiefly for transport purposes. They had already made one large cache some miles farther on.

For some fifty miles they sledged over the frozen surface of the Susitna River. This was good going. They passed an Indian village, and met one or two prospectors who had been searching for gold.

Beyond Talkeetna they left the Susitna River on their east, and followed the canyon of the Chulitna. The first thirty miles were known to them from their 1910 expedition. Their last visit had been in summer when the river raced through the canyon in a series of dangerous rapids. Now it was a smooth expanse of untrodden snow on the ice.

Progress was slow, for they had to break trail as they went, and Browne found it necessary to go ahead with a tent-pole to feel for a firm bottom through the soft surface. That night they camped in the canyon itself.

The next day they got beyond the canyon and could see Mount McKinley 'towering high into the winter sky'.

They were now in unknown country. Maps were of little use, and they were several times at a loss through not knowing the lie of the land. For instance, on one occasion Browne was ahead and found that the base of the mountains came so close to the river bank that there was hardly room for the sledges to pass. He went back and got a shovel, and managed to level the snow round the foot of the bluff, only to find that farther on was a second and steeper bluff with the river rushing round its base. There was nothing else to do but return and pioneer another route.

But there were compensations. Here is an interesting glimpse of wild life. "In all that great land there was not a sound to be heard except the creaking of my snowshoes on the dry snow. The stream I was following was spring fed. It ran deep and crystal clear and its bed was green with a kind of aquatic grass. Suddenly I heard a slight noise, and turning quickly I saw a large otter ascend the bank and stretch himself full length on the snow. He was only forty feet away, but he watched me quietly until I began to move forward, when he slipped with scarcely a ripple into the clear stream."

So day after day passed. They steadily advanced towards the source of the Chulitna and were getting anxious because so far they had not seen any pass over the Range. One day Belmore Browne went far ahead not only to break trail but to look for a possible route. The way he followed was so rocky, sometimes running between the walls of a canyon, that it was difficult to see far ahead. But he pushed on and then climbed higher, to be rewarded with the sight of an unknown river (then frozen, of course) running down from a dip in the Range and joining the Chulitna farther ahead. He hurried back with the good news, as he knew that this nameless river gave them a way over the ridge.

As they were now almost above the tree-line, they took special care in making camp that night, as afterwards they would be reduced to stoves and pemmican. Here is his description of how they made camp.

"After we had stamped down a firm foundation in the virgin snow, each man did the task required at the time. First a large dead spruce would come crashing down into the snow, followed by numerous smaller spruces. The green spruces were quickly stripped of their boughs, and the poles—we used six full lengths and four half-lengths—raised the tent. The boughs were then woven into a deep soft mattress, and a smooth foot-log placed across the tent to divide the beds from the stove and kitchen. Then the kitchen boxes were brought in, containing all the necessary foods and cooking utensils. Each man's 'war bag' and bed were placed in a row at the head of the tent; and the snow-shoes and everything else eatable—from a dog's point of view—were hung out of reach on the tent-poles. The boughs were then covered with a tarpaulin.

"While these activities were under way one of us would be sawing the dead spruce into stove lengths and splitting it, and a generous wood-pile would be ready by the time our tent was pitched.

"While the cook was at work trails would be broken to, and water brought from, the nearest water hole, and an outdoor kitchen built for cooking dog-food. More boughs were brought on which to pile our freight which was covered with our sled-covers.

"With the dog-food cooking merrily and everything outside stowed away we would repair to the tent. A rope would be stretched along the ridge-pole for our wet clothes to dry on, our beds unrolled, and we could surrender to the enjoyment of peace and warmth."

At this stage their advance was hindered by storm

"Their base camp was actually pitched at 11,000 feet up, surely the greatest height to which a dog team has been taken."

and blizzard. Driving snow and wind made it almost impossible to break a trail which the sleds and dogs could follow. But in spite of these appalling conditions, they managed to get farther up the valley which would lead them over the ridge.

On 3 April they camped at 6000 feet, and had to dig a site out of the soft snow. There they were held up by a blizzard which raged around their tent for twenty-four hours. "It was certainly a weird picture. Four men and a pack of wolf-dogs, in a storm-battered tent 6000 feet up on an icy ridge!"

The crossing of the ridge was accomplished without accident, but in their next camp, just over the north side of the Range, they were storm bound for thirty-six hours. After that the going was easier. For one thing it was downhill, though on a glacier that is not as simple as it sounds.

By 17 April they were once more amongst timber, and it is not difficult to picture their delight—wood fires once more and the protection of the trees, and more plentiful game for fresh meat.

They spent a few days enjoying the new situation, but they had to face their main task—the climbing of Mount McKinley. Their plan was to establish a base camp as high as practicable with the aid of the dogs so that they could take as much food as possible; in this way they could risk more time in the actual assault.

Their base camp was actually pitched at 11,000 feet up, surely the greatest height to which a dog team has been taken. They remained there a whole month as weather conditions were still too dangerous for risking that final climb.

From now on they had to back-pack their gear and supplies. They would have to camp out on the way and it was essential that they should have sufficient food to maintain strength.

The going was stiff. When men get above a certain height they find difficulty in breathing easily; this they expected, but they had not allowed for the depth of soft snow which made every step a labour.

They camped at 13,600 feet, and then at 15,000 feet; later at 15,800 feet and finally at 16,615 feet, the highest camp ever made in North America. In 1912 that seemed an incredible height, so it is worth noting that Camp VI on the 1933 Everest expedition was pitched at 27,400 feet.

On the morning of 29 June they set off for the final attempt on the summit towering nearly 3000 feet above them. The weather was clear, and the snow surface was hard. Browne and La Voy took it in turns to break trail, and soon this meant chopping steps in the ice; that is a laborious job, but the only way of making progress on steep slopes.

Soon after reaching 17,500 they came on a stretch of soft snow, and on the whole an icy surface is preferable to soft snow when at each step you sink in up to the knees.

By this time clouds were beginning to roll up, and the climbers watched them anxiously. Gradually the wind increased, and the sky to the south became darker, until at the base of the final peak they had to face a gale with snow driven towards them.

Their position was dangerous. If they were caught by a real blizzard it would be impossible to find their way down without running serious risk of falling into the many crevasses. However, they were in a 'now-or-never' mood, and doggedly went on chopping out steps upwards. But they did no more than about 300 feet an hour.

At about 20,000 feet the storm was in a fury and drove clouds of steel-like ice particles into their faces. The cold now was also beginning to tell upon them. Their fingers were getting numb with frost, and, as Browne said, "I was forced several times to stop and fight with desperate energy the deadly cold that was creeping up my hands and feet." Then they topped a small rise and came into the full blast of the wind. "The breath was driven from my body, and I held to my ice-axe with stooping shoulders to stand against the gale; I couldn't go ahead."

He then turned and motioned to his companions to take the slight shelter of the rocks. At last he said, "The game's up; we've got to get down." And the others had to agree that it would be suicide to go on. So they had to turn their backs on the summit and make their way through the storm back to camp. They reckoned that in clear weather, perhaps five minutes of easy walking would have taken them to the highest point.

Failure? Some may call it so, for they could not claim to be the first men to stand on the summit of Mount McKinley, but they had blazed the trail for others to follow. They had fought against Nature herself, for they recorded that "the most conservative of our estimates of the climatic conditions was a wind of 55 miles an hour, and a temperature of 15 degrees below zero".

And Browne proudly added, "Whatever we had done had been accomplished by our own unaided efforts".

VII

Cannibals and Crocodiles

CANNIBALS and crocodiles in West Africa would not attract many women however venturesome they might be, but in 1893 a young woman deliberately set off for that fever-ridden coast in order to study the habits and customs of the natives.

This bold traveller was Mary Kingsley, the niece of Charles Kingsley, author of *Westward Ho!* She had read all she could find about the adventures and discoveries of African explorers, and she had become very interested in the strange beliefs and practices of the tribes of savages who were almost untouched by civilisation.

She decided, much to the alarm of her friends, to go alone. As an excuse for her travels she set up as a trader, as she knew the natives would understand that; if she just explored they would at once get suspicious, and she knew that she would never get the information she wanted unless she could get on good terms with them.

At that time there were very few white people living on the Slave Coast, as it was significantly called; there were some traders, a good-hearted but rough lot of men, and a number of officials. There were even fewer women; wives of officials or of missionaries. They tried hard to persuade Mary Kingsley not to venture inland, but she would not be turned aside from her plan.

She had many adventures, which are recorded in her books; here it is only possible to tell you of a few, and, as far as I can, they shall be told in her own words.

First for a crocodile adventure. She spent some time paddling a small canoe in the mangrove swamps, as

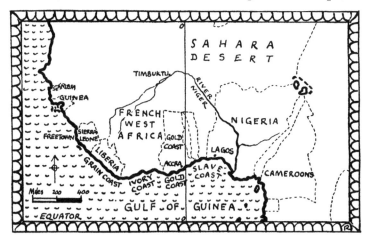

one of her interests was natural history. "On one occasion", she records, "a crocodile chose to get his front paws over the stern of my canoe, and endeavoured to improve our acquaintance. I had to retire to the bows, to keep the balance right (it is no use saying because I was frightened, for this miserably under-states the case), and fetch him a clip on the snout with a paddle, when he withdrew, and I paddled into the very middle of the lagoon, hoping the water was too deep there for him or any of his friends to repeat the performance.... This was only a pushing young creature and he had not learnt manners."

That was in her early days of adventure, and most people would have felt that such an escape was enough, but she took it all as part of the fun! Later she was to meet other wild animals and run greater risks. It should be noted that she travelled without firearms. She was once asked why she did not at least carry a revolver; she explained that she had taken one out with her from England, but there had been so much fuss about it at the Customs, that she left it behind.

Two meetings with leopards are worth giving. The first was when she was stopping in a native village. "On one occasion a big leopard had attacked a dog, who, with her family, was occupying a broken-down hut next to mine. The dog was a half-bred boarhound, and a savage brute. I, being roused by the uproar, rushed out into the feeble moonlight, thinking she was having one of her habitual turns-up with other dogs, and I saw a whirling mass of animal matter within a yard of me. I fired two mushroom-shaped native stools in rapid succession into the brown of it, and the meeting broke up into a leopard and a dog. The leopard crouched, I think to spring on me. I can see its great, beautiful eyes still, and I seized an earthen water-cooler and flung it straight at them. It was a noble shot; it burst on the leopard's head like a shell and the leopard went for the bush."

She was to have another meeting with a leopard under more trying conditions. Here is her account. "I had got caught in a tornado in a dense forest.

"It was a noble shot; it burst on the leopard's head like a shell."

The massive, mighty trees were waving like a wheat-field in an autumn gale in England, and I dare say a field mouse in a wheat-field in a gale would have heard much the same uproar. The tornado shrieked like ten thousand vengeful demons. The great trees creaked and groaned and strained against it. The fierce rain came in a roar, tearing to shreds the leaves and blossoms and deluging everything. I was making bad weather of it, and climbing up over a lot of rocks out of a gully bottom where I had been half drowned in a stream, and on getting my head to the level of a block of rock I observed right in front of my eyes, broadside on, maybe a yard off, certainly not more, a big leopard. He was crouching on the ground, with his magnificent head thrown back and his eyes shut. His fore-paws were spread out in front of him and he lashed the ground with his tail, and I grieve to say, in face of that awful danger—I don't mean me, but the tornado— he swore softly, but repeatedly and profoundly. I did not get these facts up in one glance, for no sooner did I see him than I ducked under the rocks, and remembered thankfully that leopards are said to have no power of smell. But I heard his observation on the weather, and the flip-flap of his tail on the ground. Every now and then I cautiously took a look at him with one eye round a rock-edge, and he remained in the same position. My feelings tell me he remained there twelve months, but my calmer judgment puts the time down to twenty minutes; and at last, on taking another cautious peep, I saw he was gone. It was an immense pleasure to have seen the great creature like that. He was so evidently enraged and baffled by the uproar and dazzled by the floods of lightning that swept down into the deepest recesses of the forest, showing at one second every detail of twig, leaf, branch and stone round you, and then leaving you in a sort of swirling dark until the next flash came; this, and the great conglomerate roar of wind, rain and thunder, was enough to bewilder any living thing."

From that description you will see that Mary Kingsley was not only plucky and cool-headed, but gifted with a sense of humour. It was this as much as anything else which helped her to face many dangerous and awkward situations. What would you do, for instance, if a hippopotamus got in your way? Here is what she did: "Once an hippopotamus and I were on an island alone together, and I wanted one of us to leave. I preferred it should be myself, but the hippo was close to my canoe, and looked like staying, so I made cautious and timorous advances to him and finally scratched him behind the ear with my umbrella and we parted on good terms."

The mention of her umbrella may surprise you, for it hardly seems part of the equipment needed for exploring Africa. But Mary Kingsley was a surprising woman; she dressed in Africa just as she dressed in London; long, heavy skirts and a bonnet! She claimed that the skirts saved her life on many occasions, and instanced when she accidentally fell into a pit-trap set for wild animals. "It is at these times you realise the blessing of a good thick skirt", she wrote. "If I had adopted masculine garments, I should have been spiked to the bone and done for. Whereas, save for a good many bruises, here I was with the fulness of my skirt tucked under me, sitting on nine ebony spikes some twelve inches long, in comparative comfort, howling lustily to be hauled out."

But something must be said of her trading methods. It has already been pointed out that she found the best way of getting into touch with the natives was by trading goods with them; they understood that and it explained her presence to them, whereas scientific research made them suspicious. Here is an account of one trip. She decided to visit the cannibal tribe of the Fans. She made friends with three ivory traders who were going up the Ogowé River. "They were to take me and my little belongings in their canoe to a village, and were to give me a most excellent character to the local nobility and gentry. I told them what to say, and paid them for saying it, to prevent mistakes, and then they were to leave me there and go higher up the river on their own business, and call for me on their way down. They duly took me, gave the village the idea that I was just the sort of thing to improve the local social tone, and left me. I was horribly nervous when they did, for on our way up to it we had come across a gentleman who danced and howled on the bank, and wanted to sell something badly as we were a trading company. We went for him like an arrow, thinking it might be a tooth—an elephant's I mean. It wasn't—it was a leg—not his own either, but the leg of a gentleman of some kind. This upset my companions."

No wonder she was nervous left all alone in a cannibal village! However, she started her trade next morning, and was soon busy bartering for tusks and rubber. As days went by she became anxious for the return of the other traders, as her stock of goods was getting low, and she knew that as soon as they were exhausted the Fans would begin to have fresh views of her usefulness.

"I had to start selling my own belongings, and for the first time in my life I felt the want of a big outfit. My own clothes I certainly did insist on having more for, pointing out that they were rare and curious. A dozen ladies' blouses sold well. I cannot say they looked well when worn by a brawny warrior in conjunction with nothing else but red paint and a bunch of leopard tails, particularly when the warrior failed to tie the strings at the back. But I did not hint at this, and I quite realise that a pair of stockings can be made to go further than we make them by using one at a time and putting the top part over the head and letting the rest float on the breeze. But I had too few, and they were all gone before that canoe came. The last thing I parted with was my toothbrush, and that afternoon down came the canoe just as I was making up my mind to set up in business as a witch-doctor."

Her most dangerous exploit was a journey from the Ogowé River across country to the Rembwé River; this was through the bush, which was hardly known to white men, and it was inhabited by the fiercest of the Fan tribes. Her companions were all natives from the coast, and they persuaded Fan villagers to act as guides on each stage. This arrangement had its own difficulties, for each Fan village had its feuds with the next, and as the little party approached there was some nervousness as to how they would be received.

From her account, I think it was Mary Kingsley's good humour and friendliness which got her through so many dangerous situations. Certainly the few white people on the coast hardly expected to see her return, and she was much amused by the gloomy way in which they said goodbye to her.

Here is a glimpse of the kind of country they were going through. "Our second day's march was infinitely worse than the first, for it lay along a series of abruptly shaped hills with deep ravines between them; each ravine had its swamp and each swamp its river. The large swamps were best to deal with, because they made a break in the forest, and the sun can come down on their surface and bake a crust, over which you can go, if you go quickly. The Fans went across all right with a rapid striding glide, but the other men erred from excess of caution, and while hesitating as to where was the next safe place to plant their feet, the place that they were standing on went in with a glug. Moreover, they would keep together, which was more than the crust would stand. Two gave us a fine job in one bog by sinking in close together. Some of us slashed off boughs of trees and tore handfuls of hard canna leaves, while others threw them round the sinking victims to form a sort of raft, and then with the aid of bushrope they were hauled out."

But they found that the worst kind of swamp was the

deep, narrow one which was always shaded from the sun, and so was simply liquid mud. Then the one in front had to try here and there for a ford, and this meant sometimes getting in above the waist. Mary Kingsley hated doing this, and no one can be surprised at that, for all kinds of snakes and crawling things loved such slimy places. But if she happened to be in front, she took her turn at finding a ford, for as she put it, she dared not show 'the white feather at anything that turned up'.

Occasionally they came to ravines spanned by primitive bridges, made of bushropes, that is strong creepers, or of a tree-trunk just dropped across. The following incident brings out very clearly the spirit of the woman and of her companions.

"Across the bottom of the steep ravine, from one side to the other, lay an enormous tree as a bridge, about fifteen feet above the river, which rushed beneath it, over a boulder-encumbered bed. I took in the situation at once, and then and there I would have changed that bridge for any swamp I have ever seen, yea, even for a certain bushrope bridge in which I once wound myself like a buzzing fly in a spider's web. I was fearfully tired, and my legs shivered under me after the falls of the previous part of the day, and my boots were slippery with water soaking.

"The Fans went into the river, and half swam, half waded across. All the Ajumba (coast natives), save Pagan, followed, and Ngouta got across with their assistance. Pagan thought he would try the bridge, and I thought I would watch how the thing worked.

He got about three yards along it and then slipped, but caught the tree with his hands as he fell, and hauled himself back to my side again; then he went down the bank and through the water. This was not calculated to improve one's nerve; I knew by now I had got to go by the bridge, for I saw I was not strong enough in my tired state to fight the water. If only the wretched thing had had its bark on it would have been better, but it was bare, and bald, and round, and a slip meant death on the rocks below. I rushed it, and reached the other side in safety, whereby poor Pagan got chaffed about his failure by the others, who said they had gone through the water just to wash their feet.

"The other side, when we got there, did not seem much worth reaching, being a swampy fringe at the bottom of a steep hillside, and after a few yards the path turned into a stream or backwater of the river. It was hedged with thick bushes, and covered with water on top of semi-liquid mud. Now and again for a change you had a foot of water on top of a fearfully slippery harder mud, and then we light-heartedly took headers into the bush, sideways, or sat down; and when it was not proceeding on the evil tenor of its way, like this, it had holes in it; in fact, I fancy the bottom of the holes was the true level, for it came near to being as full of holes as a fishing-net, and it was very quaint to see the man in front, who had been paddling along knee-deep before, now plop down with the water round his shoulders; and getting out of these slippery pockets, which were sometimes a tight fit, was difficult. However, that is the path you have got to go by, if you're not wise enough to stop at home."

Her cheerful way of relating her adventures may make us overlook the very real hardships she had to suffer, and the amazing bravery she showed under conditions which many an experienced explorer would avoid if possible. So also we may forget that all this time she was collecting information about the native customs and collecting rare plants and animal specimens.

She is now remembered for the good work she did on her return to England in urging a better way of treating the natives, and her enthusiasm resulted in many reforms of policy in West Africa.

When the Boer War broke out, she decided to go to South Africa and offer her services to the Army authorities. They were glad of her help, and she was soon nursing the sick and wounded with the same cheerfulness that she had shown in her travels.

Unhappily she caught a fever, and died in 1900 after two months' work. They buried her at sea according to her wish. Her death was a great loss, for her work in and for West Africa was not finished, but she leaves a name as a most fearless explorer.

VIII

The Camp of Death

FEW men would choose a desert for exploration. It offers no excitement or surprises, and it may mean a lingering death from thirst. Yet men have even risked that for the sake of knowledge.

The Swedish explorer, Sven Hedin, spent many years in Central Asia during the latter part of last century. A map showing the routes he followed looks like a spider's web as the lines cross and recross in all directions. But he escaped death by a hair's breadth on one occasion when he crossed the Taklamakan Desert.

This lies to the north-west of that land of mystery we call Tibet. It is bounded by two rivers, the Yarkand and the Khotan. From Lailik, Hedin's base, on the Yarkand, straight across it is about 200 miles. A well provisioned caravan would not be running unusual risks in making the journey, but unfortunately for Hedin he relied on a man who failed him.

They had eight carefully chosen camels. A supply of 100 gallons of water was taken in tanks; this Hedin estimated would last at least twenty-five days, and he hoped to make the crossing in not more than fifteen days. Food supplies were calculated on the same generous basis.

He decided not to take a direct route, but to bear north-east towards the hill country of Masar-tagh. The sand would be firmer than in the centre of the desert, and they could hope to camp in comfort when they got to the hills.

All seemed to smile on them as they set out. The weather was springlike and Hedin expected a somewhat monotonous journey over the bare country. He little knew what lay ahead!

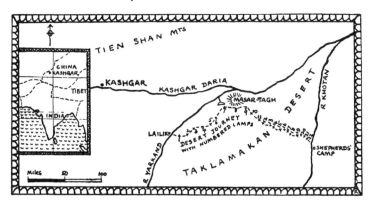

As far as the Masar-tagh all went well apart from the usual incidents such as camels slipping their loads, or breaking loose. At each camp a well was dug and this gave water for the beasts though it was too brackish to be enjoyable for human drinking.

Camp 7 was particularly delightful. Hedin called it an earthly paradise. They were amongst trees and the near-by lake and streams gave plenty of water. So pleasant was it that they rested a day and overhauled their equipment.

Hedin consulted with his men. Yollchi, his caravan leader, assured him that from that camp they were only about four days' march from the River Khotan. The only map, an old one, suggested that the distance was greater than this, so Hedin to be on the safe side assumed that they would have at least six days of desert travel. To be even safer he ordered Yollchi to see that at least ten days' water was taken in the tanks.

The next day they turned their backs on Masar-tagh and the real desert journey began. The going was difficult. We often think of a desert as a flat plain of sand, but more often the surface is a mass of dunes running to a height of 60 or even 100 feet. If you have ever walked among sand-dunes by the sea, you can imagine the difficulties of getting loaded camels along.

As far as possible they kept to the ridges to avoid going up and down the slopes of soft sand, but this also meant that they could not take a direct course but zigzagged about in order to make the going easier.

Here is Hedin's own description of what he felt as they penetrated into the desert.

"A strange feeling came over me when I encamped in the dreariest desert there is on the face of the earth. The men spoke but little; not one of them laughed. An unwonted silence reigned around the little fire of tamarisk roots. We tethered the camels for the night close to our sleeping-place, to prevent them from breaking loose and going back to the lake. A death-like silence held us all under its spell. The only sound to be heard was the heavy, long-drawn, measured breathing of the camels."

Sandstorms made their journey more difficult. The

sand got everywhere; they breathed it as they travelled and ate it with their food. It got down into their clothes and rubbed the skin in an irritating way.

"The camels", Hedin records, "were visibly tiring. Heavy falls grew more and more frequent. When they fell on a steep incline, they were unable to get up without help. One of the beasts, which came down near the summit of a ridge, we were obliged to free entirely from his burden, saddle and all; and then, all putting our shoulders to him, we rolled him seventy feet down the slope into a hollow between two sand-dunes. It was only then that he was able to recover his feet."

They were only doing about eight miles a day then, and a glance at the map shows how the camp-sites got closer and closer as the journey progressed.

It was at Camp 12 that Hedin made an alarming discovery. He examined the water tanks and found that there was only water left for two days. He sent for Yollchi and asked why his orders for ten days' water supply had not been carried out. But Yollchi was quite certain there was nothing to worry about.

'It is only four days' journey from the lake to the next watering place. We must soon be there.'

This reassured Hedin, as Yollchi was supposed to know the route, but he gave orders that every care was to be taken of what water was left.

Then the first of the camels broke down, and had to be abandoned. From that time till the end Hedin walked with the others to save the camels as much as possible.

They had hoped that the dunes would get lower and that they would reach flatter ground. But a chaos of ridges and hollows presented itself. Some of the dunes even rose to a height of more than a hundred feet, and up and down these they had to travel.

In camp they dug a well and managed to get a little brackish water. This revived man and beast, and renewed their hopes. Each night they expected to see the Khotan the following day.

Camp 14 was pitched and again they tried for water, but this time the lower they dug the drier the sand became. An inspection of the tanks showed that there was very little water left; with care, enough for one day.

Two more camels had collapsed on the way and had to be left, and gradually any gear which could be spared was abandoned.

One day was made more terrible by a sand-storm of the kind which is called 'black' because it is so dense that it turns day into night. Slowly they moved forward keeping closely to each other. When more violent gusts came the men crouched on the ground or hid their faces in the sides of the camels.

The men behaved well except for Yollchi, who on one occasion was caught stealing water; for this he was all but murdered by the others before Hedin intervened. They had one-third of a pint left! They moistened their lips and then divided the rest amongst them as equally as possible.

Hedin himself was beginning to lose strength, and it was only with the greatest difficulty that he managed to get along. One of the men became delirious; the camels could hardly move with any load.

They decided to change their method of journeying, and to rest in the heat of the day and move forward in the cooler evening. The temptation to lie down and wait for death was almost too strong, but with the setting of the sun, and on one day, with the rise of a cool breeze, they recovered energy to push forward.

Camp 18 was named 'The Camp of Death', for it was there that they left everything except bare necessities. There too they had to leave Yollchi and another of their comrades in the tent in the faint hope that they might somehow be able to return for them. Hedin went forward with two men, Islam Bai and Kasim, and the remaining camels.

Poor beasts, their strength slowly ebbed away. Late that night staggering forward the caravan came to a stop because the camels could go no farther. Islam Bai too broke down. What was to be done?

Hedin and Kasim decided to go on until they dropped. The Khotan *must* be near, and once they reached that they could perhaps help the others. Their hopes were vague; there was really only one thing which occupied their thoughts—they must find water.

The next two days were a nightmare. They carried what food they could; but so parched were their throats that they could not swallow. Their other important burden was a spade. It seems an absurd tool to carry in the desert on a forlorn hope, but with it they could dig on the chance of getting water. It also served to dig their beds.

"In the faint hope that they might somehow be able to return for them."

They had no tent of course and the surface of the sand was so hot that sleeping on it during the day was out of the question. They solved the problem by stripping and burying themselves in the sand low enough to reach the cooler layers underneath. They hung their clothes over the spade to give a little shade.

"Thus", wrote Hedin, "we lay buried alive in the eternal sand, uttering never a word, and yet not able to sleep. We did not move until six o'clock in the evening; then we got out of our sand-bath, dressed, and continued our journey at a slow and heavy pace, for in all probability the dry sand-bath had weakened us. Nevertheless, we stuck to it doggedly, although we had innumerable stoppages, pushing on eastwards, ever eastwards, until one o'clock next morning."

Towards the end of their second day's journey their hopes were revived by reaching a tamarisk tree—the first green they had seen for some time, and a herald of water. Other tamarisks dotted the landscape. They tried digging for water, but they had not enough strength; the spade turned in their hands.

Later they sighted a poplar tree—this gave them more hope.

That hope faded the next day as once more the dunes began, and as they stumbled down the slopes all sight of trees was lost. For ten hours of the greatest heat they lay stretched out at the foot of a tamarisk.

Kasim was fast losing his strength. As the cooler evening came, Hedin roused himself for another effort. Kasim made a feeble gesture that he could not move.

Hedin went on alone. His strength too was ebbing, but he was determined to find water; it was their one faint chance of life.

After going a few hours, resting time and time again, he at length sank down exhausted and dosed. Presently he was wakened by the sound of footsteps. It was Kasim who had managed to pull himself together and had followed him.

They tottered on in the dark night, and after an hour had passed they were surprised to see footprints in the sand. This roused them completely.

'They must be the footprints of some shepherd', suggested Hedin.

Kasim was examining the track carefully. Then he turned and said in a voice of despair, 'They are our own!' It was true. There was the mark of the spade which Kasim used as a support. This was almost the last straw, but after a few hours of rest, they once more went on.

They were at length rewarded by seeing in the distance a line of trees. It was without question the forest which lined the banks of the Khotan. They were saved if only they could get that far.

They made their slow way over a stretch of barren sand, and at long last entered the wood. They threw themselves down in the shade and panted after their exertions. A few hours' rest were necessary, but when Hedin got up he found that Kasim was beaten at last. He shook his head at his leader and by feeble signs urged him to go on, drink, and bring back water to him. Hedin settled him as comfortably as possible.

He took off the blade of the spade and hung it in one of the trees so that he could find the spot on his return. Then with the shaft as a support he set off.

What followed is best told in his own words.

"It was anything but easy work. Two or three times I very nearly got stuck fast in the thorny bushes. I tore my clothes and scratched my hands. I rested on roots and fallen tree-trunks; I was fearfully tired. It cost me inconceivable efforts to keep awake. Then all at once the forest came to an end, and to the east stretched a dead level plain of hard clay and sand. It lay five or six feet below the level of the forest. It could not possibly be anything but the bed of the Khotan. But the sand was as dry as the sand in the desert dunes. The river-bed was empty, waiting for the summer floods to come down from the mountains. It was inconceivable that I should perish in the very bed of the river I had been so long and so desperately seeking. I resolved to cross over to the other side before I gave up all hope.

"Leaning on the spade-shaft, I plodded away at a steady pace in a straight line as though I were being led by an unseen hand. At intervals I was seized by a traitorous desire to sleep, and was obliged to stop and rest. My pulse was weak; I could scarcely discern its beats. I had to steel myself by the strongest efforts of will to prevent myself from dropping off to sleep. I was afraid that if I did go off, I should never waken again."

"After going about a mile and a half, I was at length able to distinguish the dark line of the forest on the right bank of the river. I was only a few yards from the bank when a wild-duck flew up and away. I heard a splash, and in the next moment I stood on the brink of a little pool filled with fresh, cool water."

He drank and drank, and then bathed his hands and face in the wonderful water. Strength flowed back into his body.

His next thought was of Kasim. He filled his gumboots with water and slung them on the spade-shaft like a yoke and set off back.

The rest of the story can soon be told. Kasim too was quickly revived with the water, and after they had had a well-needed sleep in the shadow of the forest, they made for the river-bed.

After some wandering, they came across a shepherd's camp on the other side of the river. There they were taken care of, and a rescue party set off. They found Islam Bai and one camel, but when they reached Camp 18, there was no living man or beast: it was indeed 'The Camp of Death'.

IX

Finding Robinson Crusoe

On 1 October 1711 two small ships anchored off Erith; they were laden with valuable treasure taken from enemy ships, but on one of them was Robinson Crusoe himself. That was not his name, but Alexander Selkirk's experiences gave Daniel Defoe the idea for the story you all know.

The two ships were the *Duke* (320 tons) and the *Dutchess* (260 tons). They were under the command of Captain Woodes Rogers. In August 1708 they had sailed from Bristol with a commission from the Government to attack any French or Spanish ships they might meet, as England was then at war with those two nations. Such roving ships with Government commissions were called privateers.

They sailed by way of the Canary Islands and the Cape Verde Islands to the coast of Brazil, and on 19 November they anchored off the Island of Grande. There they stayed for about a month, overhauling the ships and reprovisioning them, and at the same time giving the sailors (there were some 300 of them) the chance of a spell ashore. In those days it was necessary for ships to break long voyages in this manner, for their means of preserving food were primitive, and life on board was by no means healthy.

Their next plan was to sail into the Pacific round Cape Horn, and put in at the islands of Juan Fernandez for fresh water and another rest. The distance from Grande to the islands was nearly 6000 miles.

You are sure to have heard of the dangers of sailing round the south of South America. The seas are stormy, and the wind is generally blowing hard from the west, and a ship sailing from the Atlantic into the Pacific expects to have a rough passage.

Here are some extracts from the sea-journal kept by Captain Woodes Rogers at this time. He was himself on the *Duke*, and had with him Captain William Dampier, the famous ex-buccaneer, who was then employed by the Government for his skill as a navigator.

"*Jan.* 5 (1709). Just past twelve Yesterday it came on to blow strong: We got down our Fore-Yard, and reef'd our Fore-Sail and Main-Sail; but there came on a violent Gale of Wind, and a great Sea. A little before six we saw the *Dutchess* lowering her Main-Yard: the Tack flew up, and the Lift unreev'd, so that the Sail to Leeward was in the water and all a-back, their Ship took in a great deal of Water to Leeward; immediately they loos'd their Sprit-Sail, and wore her before the Wind: I wore after her, and came as near as I could to 'em, expecting when they had gotten their Main-Sail stow'd they would take another Reef in, and bring to again under a two-reef'd Main-Sail, and reef'd and ballanc'd Mizen, if the Ship would not keep to without it: but to my surprize they kept scudding to the Southward. I dreaded running amongst Ice, because it was excessive cold; so I fir'd a Gun as a Signal for them to bring to, and brought to our selves

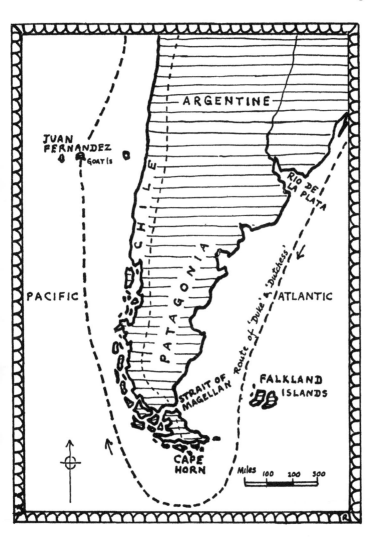

again under the same reef'd Main-Sail. They kept on, and our Men on the look-out told me they had an Ensign in their Maintop-Mast Shrouds as a Signal of Distress, which made me doubt they had sprung their Main-Mast; so I wore again, our Ship working exceeding well in this great Sea. Just before night I was up with them again, and set our Fore-Sail twice reef'd to keep 'em Company, which I did all night. About three this morning it grew more moderate; we soon after made a Signal to speak with them, and at five they brought to: when I came within haile, I enquir'd how they all did aboard; they answer'd, they had ship'd a great deal of Water in lying by, and were forc'd to put before the Wind, and the Sea had broke in the Cabin-Windows, and over their Stern, filling their Steerage and Waste, and had like to have spoil'd several Men; but God be thank'd all was otherwise indifferent well with 'em, only they were intolerably cold, and every thing wet. At ten we made sail, Wind at WNW. and moderate. Lat. 60.58.

"*Jan.* 6. Raw cold Weather, with some Rain. A great Sea from the NW. little Wind from the NNW. to the West. I and Capt. *Dampier* went in the Yall on board the *Dutchess*, to visit 'em after this Storm; where we found 'em in a very orderly pickle, with all their Clothes drying, the Ship and Rigging cover'd with them from the Deck to the Main-Top: They got six more Guns into the Hold, to make the Ship lively.

"*Jan.* 7. Fresh Gales of Wind, with hazy Weather and some small Rain. Yesterday about three in the Afternoon *John Veale* a Landman died, having lain ill a Fortnight, and had a Swelling in his Legs ever since he left *Grande*. At nine last night we bury'd him; this is the first that died by Sickness out of both Ships since we left *England*. Several of the *Dutchess's* Men had contracted Illness by the Wet and Cold. Wind from the NNW. to the WNW.

"*Jan.* 10. Strong Gales of Wind, with Squalls of Rain and Hail, and a great Sea from the W. We lay by with our Head to the Southward till 12 last night, then came to sail under three-reef'd Courses, and sometimes the Maintop-Sail low set, Wind from the W. to the N. and thence to the NW. We have no Night here. Lat. 61.53. Long. W. from *Lond.* 79.58 being the furthest we run this way, and for ought we know the furthest that any one has yet been to the Southward.

"*Jan.* 14. Moderate Gales with cloudy Weather, Wind veerable. This day the *Dutchess* bury'd a Man that died of the Scurvy.

"*Jan.* 15. Cloudy Weather, with Squalls of Rain, fresh Gales at SW. We had an Observ. Lat. 56 S. We now account ourselves in the *South-Sea*, being got round Cape *Horne*. The *French* Ships that came first to trade in these Seas came thro' the Straits of *Magellan*: but Experience has taught them since, that it is the best Passage to go round Cape *Horne*, where they have Sea-room enough; the Straits, being in many places very narrow, with strong Tides and no Anchor-ground."

That is how a seaman in the eighteenth century recorded his experiences; you will have noticed that his writing and spelling are not quite the same as ours, and even if you do not understand all the nautical terms, you will get a good impression of the dangers of rounding The Horn.

He gives their most southerly point as 61.53 degrees latitude, and this was, as he thought, probably a record for those days. Indeed had they gone a little farther south, they might have discovered Graham Land more than a hundred years before it was actually added to the map.

They now gladly made sail northwards for the islands of Juan Fernandez; there they proposed staying for a time in order that the ships could be overhauled and the men get a much needed change by living on shore with fresh water and fresh meat.

Dampier had visited the islands in his buccaneering days, but records of the longitude and latitude varied so much that they thought they had missed them; but on 31 January the islands were sighted.

That night they were startled to see a light on the larger of the two islands. They thought it must be from a French ship, so they cleared for action and waited for morning to dawn.

It was not an easy business getting close inshore on account of the sudden gusts of wind from the land which arose from time to time, but at last they anchored in a bay. There was no sign of enemy ships. Woodes Rogers decided that they must have slipped away at night; the real explanation of the mysterious light did not come until a boat's crew had landed. Then they met "a Man cloth'd in Goat-Skins, who look'd wilder than the first Owners of them".

This man was Alexander Selkirk, the original Robinson Crusoe. In the story you will remember that the hero spends "eight and twenty years all alone in an uninhabited island on the coast of America, near the mouth of the great River of Oronooque". Daniel Defoe did not copy Alexander Selkirk's adventures in detail; thus he puts the island off the east coast of America and not the west, but, as you will see from the following account, he got many useful ideas from the 'Man cloth'd in Goat-Skins'.

Alexander Selkirk had spent four and a quarter years on his island; he had been Master of a ship called the *Cinque-Ports*, and having quarrelled with his Captain, was put ashore on one of the islands of Juan Fernandez. He had hoped that he would soon be taken off by an English ship, but more than four years passed before the arrival of Woodes Rogers.

When he landed Selkirk had with him, "Clothes and Bedding, with a Firelock, some Powder, Bullets, and Tobacco, a Hatchet, a Knife, a Kettle, a Bible, some practical Pieces (i.e. a few tools), and his Mathematical Instruments and Books". He built two huts with branches and covered them with long grass. Later he lined them with goat-skins, for there were many of these animals on the island, and you will recall what good use Robinson Crusoe made of them. His powder was soon finished, so he learned to make fire by rubbing two sticks together. He spent much of his time "in reading, singing Psalms, and praying; so that he said he was a better Christian while in this

Solitude than ever he was before, or than, he was afraid, he should ever be again".

Food became a serious problem. Lack of bread and salt were what he felt most of all. Once his powder was exhausted he had to find other means of capturing goats for food, and later to supply him with skins. This is how he got over his difficulty.

"When his Powder fail'd, he took them (the goats) by speed of foot; for his way of living and continual Exercise of walking and running, clear'd him of all gross Humours, so that he ran with wonderful Swiftness thro the Woods and up the Rocks and Hills, as we perceiv'd when we employ'd him to catch Goats for us. We had a Bull-Dog, which we sent with several of our nimblest Runners, to help him in catching Goats; but he distanc'd and tir'd both the Dog and the Men, catch'd the Goats, and brought 'em to us on his back. He told us that his agility in pursuing a Goat had once like to have cost him his Life; he pursu'd it with so much Eagerness that he catch'd hold of it on the brink of a Precipice, of which he was not aware, the Bushes having hid it from him; so that he fell with the Goat down the said Precipice a great height, and was so stun'd and bruis'd with the Fall, that he narrowly escap'd with his Life, and when he came to his Senses, found the Goat dead under him. He lay there about 24 hours, and was scarce able to crawl to his Hutt, which was about a mile distant, or to stir abroad again in ten days."

The island had been used for some years as a useful place for ships to get fresh water, but during the whole

"He distanc'd and tir'd both the dog and the men, catch'd the goats, and brought 'em to us on his back."

of Selkirk's stay the only ships to call had been two Spanish ones; these he avoided, as to be captured by the Spaniards would he knew mean imprisonment. One result of these occasional visits was that there were a lot of rats on the island which were a pest; fortunately there were also a few cats, and by taming these Selkirk managed to keep the rats at bay, though the official version is hard to believe, for it reads, "the Rats gnaw'd his Feet and Clothes while asleep, which oblig'd him to cherish the Cats with his Goats-flesh; by which many of them became so tame, that they would lie about him in *hundreds*, and soon deliver'd him from the Rats".

He had soon worn out his shoes, and after living for several years without anything to cover his feet, he found it almost impossible to wear shoes and preferred to go barefooted.

He made his clothes out of goat-skins, stitching them together with thongs with a nail as his only needle. A new knife was contrived out of some old iron left by one ship; he beat the iron thin and then sharpened it on a stone. He was certainly not quite as fortunate as Robinson Crusoe in the things saved from the wreck; in fact Crusoe was too lucky compared with his original.

When Selkirk met his countrymen, they could hardly understand his speech, for he had got out of the habit of talking aloud. Another problem was that of food. At first he could not relish the ship's provisions, and he had lost his liking for rum—much to the amazement of the sailors.

Woodes Rogers appointed Selkirk second mate on the *Duke*. The ships remained at the island for a fortnight; it was a busy time. Sick men were landed and put into tents; sails were repaired, and all gear overhauled. By 14 February everything was ready for the next stage of the voyage.

One of their objects was to capture the Spanish treasure ships which annually sailed to Spain from America. Ever since the time of Drake these ships had been regarded as lawful prizes for any English ship. Rogers did not succeed in capturing the greatest of the vessels, but he seized one and seriously injured another. The loot captured was considerable.

They carried out their privateering work off the west coast of North America, and not only captured ships but attacked towns and held them to ransom. Then, laden with loot, they set sail for the East India Islands. The distance was about 6000 miles, and on an average they did one hundred miles a day. Provisions got very low and there was much sickness before they eventually anchored off Batavia in Java.

After the usual rest, they set sail for the Cape, and arrived there at the end of December 1710. Another ten months brought them home after their voyage round the world.

There was much public enthusiasm about the success of the venture, for the plunder was estimated to be worth over half a million, but there was even greater curiosity to see Alexander Selkirk and hear of his strange experiences.

Since then a memorial to him has been erected on

his look-out hill on Goat Island, the larger of the two
called Juan Fernandez. It reads thus:

In Memory
of
ALEXANDER SELKIRK
Mariner

A native of Largo, in the County of Fife, Scot-
land, who lived on this island in complete
solitude for 4 years and 4 months. He was landed
from the *Cinque-Ports* galley, 96 tons, 18 guns, A.D.
1704, and was taken off in the *Duke*, privateer,
12th February, 1709. He died Lieutenant of
H.M.S. *Weymouth*, A.D. 1721, aged 47.

X

Bird-nesting in the Antarctic

MEN will suffer untold misery for the sake of strange things. Here is the story of three men who endured all the discomforts and perils of a winter journey in the Antarctic for the sake of getting three eggs! Their names were Edward Wilson, H. R. Bowers, and Apsley Cherry-Garrard, three members of Scott's Last Expedition of 1910–13.

The record of Scott's heroic journey to the South Pole with its tragic end has become part of the tradition of our race, and men will never tire of hearing it retold. But the very nobility of that story has tended to make us overlook other journeys which were made for scientific purposes during the same period. Amongst these the bird-nesting expedition led by Wilson ranks high as a great achievement.

The idea of the journey was Wilson's. He wanted to find out more about the Emperor Penguin, and especially about its eggs and breeding habits. Now there was only one known rookery of this particular kind of Penguin; it was situated at Cape Crozier.

The difficulty was that these birds—for they are birds in spite of looking like Aldermen at a Corporation Banquet—breed in the late winter, and at that period in the Antarctic there is very little daylight. No party had so far dared a night journey across those frozen wastes; but Wilson wanted those eggs so badly that he was prepared to take the risk, and the other two men went for the fun of it.

The Winter Hut—where the expedition was settled —was at Cape Evans some 70 miles from Cape Crozier. That does not seem very far, but the route had its own problems. The Cape is at the south-east corner of

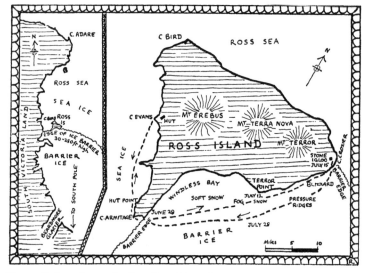

Ross Island, and the Ice Barrier extends all along its southern shore. This Barrier is constantly changing, and the pressure it exerts on the land in its movements pushes up great ridges of ice and snow which make the area dangerous. In daylight that danger is small, for it is possible to pick out a good route and avoid the worst places with their crevasses. But without light there are constant risks. And you must remember that almost throughout this journey they were travelling in the dark. The moon helped a bit, and later on the approaching dawn of summer made things easier.

So these three men set off, towards the end of June. They had two 9 foot sledges and their total gear and supplies weighed nearly 800 lb.

They soon found that night conditions made a great difference to sledging. Everything had to be done more slowly—this was due to the intense cold which sapped their energy. After a few days they gave up troubling to distinguish between day and night, but just carried on with stretches of sledging sandwiched between bouts of sleep.

Their greatest problem was that everything froze so quickly. Sleeping-bags became one mass of ice, and had to be thawed out before it was possible to get into them. Their breath froze into a solid sheet which glued their headgear on to their heads, and it was not until the Primus stove had been going for some time in the tent that they could get their heads free.

Once outside the tent in the morning they just got 'iced-up', and if they stood still for a minute they became frozen stiff. It sounds unbelievable, but here is what Cherry-Garrard himself says: "We had had our breakfast, struggled into our foot-gear, and squared up inside the tent, which was comparatively warm. Once outside I raised my head to look round and found I could not move it back. My clothing had frozen hard as I stood—perhaps fifteen seconds. For four hours I had to pull with my head stuck up, and from that time we all took care to bend down into a pulling position before being frozen in."

One serious danger they had to watch—frozen feet. It was not always easy to tell whether their feet were frozen or not, for they soon lost all feeling in them. Wilson fortunately was a doctor, and so they described the condition of their feet to him, and if he decided that it sounded serious, they immediately camped.

Temperatures were fantastic. At the end of June the thermometer registered minus 50 degrees during the day, falling at night to minus 66 degrees. "They talk of chattering teeth," wrote Cherry-Garrard, "but when your whole body chatters you may call yourself cold." The lowest temperature they recorded was on 5 July, when the thermometer showed minus 77·5 degrees, or 109½ degrees of frost.

Another trouble was blisters; they got these on their hands through the necessary rough handling of sledges and gear. The matter in the blisters froze into ice during the day. You can imagine how painful that was when pulling on a sledge rope or helping to fasten the tent door.

All the time the darkness made matters worse, and got on their nerves. Cherry-Garrard invented a formula which he repeated to himself as he went along. It was, "You've got it in the neck—stick it—stick it—you've got it in the neck." That helped a lot, he said.

The first stage of the journey, from the Winter Hut to Hut Point, was done without unusual difficulty as regards pulling the sledges, but once they were round Hut Point they came into a bay where snow conditions were abominable. The surface was just like sand,

and to pull the sledges through it was a wearisome business.

There is a curious reason for this soft snow. This particular bay rarely gets any wind. Now wind will harden a snow surface, but since the air in this bay was always calm, the snow never got hardened and so remained powdery.

On 30 June they were advancing into the bay, but soon found that they could not haul both sledges at once. They had to adopt a most curious method of progress. They took one sledge a distance, and then trudged back for the second. Now during the middle hours of the day there was just sufficient dim light for them to make out their own footprints for each return journey; they could not see the other sledge. But when that faint glimmering of light failed, they carried a lighted candle to find the way. It must have looked a queer sight.

They progressed just over three miles that day, but actually they had walked ten miles through having to make the double journey. Fortunately for a few days there was no wind as they crossed the bay, and later the moon rose and gave just enough light for them to do without their candle. Travelling was slow, and on one day they did barely more than two miles in eight hours of hard work.

Can you imagine how monotonous a journey can be when you cannot see where you are going? There was, however, one sight which helped to improve matters; the Aurora Australis was always before them. It can best be described perhaps as a low arch hanging

in the sky with coloured streamers like a fringe droop-
ing and swaying from it. This beautiful phenomenon
was in front of them on their outward journey.

On 3 July they had a pleasant surprise; the temperature rose to minus 27 degrees, but the wind had got
up, and snow was steadily falling. This fresh snow made
progress all but impossible.

Several times Wilson asked his companions whether
they would prefer to go back as the conditions were so
awful. But they wanted to go on, though they realised
what they were risking. One day they managed only
1½ miles after incredible labour.

A new difficulty presented itself about 8 July in the
form of fog; this again made for slow progress, but by
this time they were on a firmer surface and could now
draw the two sledges at once; so what they lost in one
way, they gained in another.

By 12 July they were off Terror Point, and were approaching the pressure ridges—which they could not
see. Now, too, they were in danger of crevasses, and
the rest of the outward journey is described by Cherry-
Garrard as "days of blindman's buff with the Emperor
Penguins among the crevasses of Cape Crozier".

Then they heard the noise of the pressure as the ice
pushed itself against the land.

"*Bang*—right under our feet. More bangs, and
creaks and groans; for that ice was moving and splitting
like glass. The cracks went off all round us, and some
of them ran along for hundreds of yards. Afterwards
we got used to it, but at first the effect was very
jumpy."

When they turned in on 10 July they noticed that the temperature was steadily rising; snow was again falling and visibility was nil. These signs suggested that a storm might be blowing up. By the morning there was a blizzard, and the temperature actually rose to plus 9 degrees. For three days they were forced to remain in their tent. The change was not unwelcome. They were warmer, and all the ice melted out of their clothes. "We lay steaming and beautifully liquid, and wondered sometimes what we should be like when our gear froze up once more."

At last on 13 July they were able to continue their journey as the storm had died down. But it took several hours of hard work to dig out the tent and the sledges.

That day they did a good run—over seven miles, and a faint moon made things easier; it certainly helped them to avoid one large crevasse which might have swallowed men and sledges. Two days later they reached Cape Crozier.

Their plan was to build a snow-hut or igloo up on the shore during their stay as this would be more roomy and comfortable than the tent. Then they could climb down to the penguin rookery and make their observations and get the eggs.

The building of the igloo was an interesting job. They made the walls of rocks and stones, banked up with snow. Across the top they placed one of the sledges, and over it and the wall tops stretched a large piece of canvas they had brought for the purpose; they had even carried along with them a piece of board to make a lintel over the doorway.

The weather was not too troublesome though the wind was at times rather gusty and strong. But by 20 July the hut was made, and the tent pitched near it, and used for their stores and spare gear.

The penguin rookery was about four miles away, and it was by no means a simple business climbing round the Cape and then down to the barrier edge. On their first—and as it proved their only—expedition to the penguins they got five eggs, but two of these got broken before they were back in the igloo.

By now the weather was getting thicker, and the outlook far from promising. They kept saying to each other, 'Things must improve', but Nature replied by showing that they could get very much worse.

It was during the night of 21 July that the climax came. This is how Cherry-Garrard describes it.

"It was blowing as though the world was having a fit of hysterics. The earth was torn in pieces; the indescribable fury and roar of it all cannot be imagined. 'Bill, Bill, the tent has gone', was the next I remember —from Bowers shouting at us again and again through the door."

At the moment they did not stop to consider the seriousness of their position, but fought their way out into the blinding snow-storm to rescue whatever gear they could. Very little was lost, and when they struggled back into the igloo, they were able to sort things out and take stock of their prospects.

There they were, three men in the darkness of an Antarctic winter, storm bound, with only a limited amount of food and fuel, *without a tent*. But even worse

"On their first—and as it proved their only—expedition to the penguins they got five eggs."

was in store for them. The wind raged round them
without any sign of lessening its force. Gradually the
igloo began to show signs of weakening against these
unending attacks. They stuffed everything they could
into the cracks in the walls, but the snow was forced
in and they were getting drifted up.

Then the roof-canvas went. "The top of the door
opened in little slits, and that green Willesden canvas
flapped into hundreds of little fragments in fewer
seconds than it takes to read this. Even above the
savage thunder of that great wind on the mountain
came the lash of the canvas as it whipped to little tiny
strips. The highest rocks which we had built into our
walls fell upon us, and a sheet of drift came in."

Somehow they managed to get into their sleeping-
bags—the only secure things now which remained to
them, apart from the flooring of canvas underneath
them.

"There was so much to worry about that there was
not the least use in worrying; and we were so *very* tired.
And so we lay, wet and quite fairly warm, hour after
hour while the wind roared round us, blowing storm
force continually and rising in gusts to something indescribable."

For three days they were unable to move. Then
there was a lessening in the weather, and they decided
to try to get a meal. They got the floor-cloth wedged
between their sleeping-bags, and then drew it over
their heads. With that shelter, they got the Primus
going. It took a long time to melt the snow and get
things hot enough, but "in time we got both tea and

pemmican, which was full of hairs from our bags, penguin feathers, dirt and debris, but delicious".

Then they decided to search for the tent. They all felt that this was a hopeless business, but it was a chance worth taking. Bowers went off down the slope, and Wilson and Cherry-Garrard followed slowly. Presently they were startled to hear Bowers calling to them farther down the steep slope. They went after him, and found him with the tent!

It had been lifted up like an umbrella, but the bamboo ribs had closed up, and there it was safe and sound. You can imagine their feelings. It was literally a reprieve from death, and they knew it. They carefully carried it up the slope again, and pitched it more securely than any tent had ever been pitched before. "If that tent went again we were going with it."

Then they had a good hot meal; collected all the gear, and settled in for a night's rest, for the next morning they were going to set off back. All possibility of seeing more of the penguins had vanished.

They made fair progress, though the wind was still strong and held them up for some hours. By the end of 26 July they were clear of the pressure ridges, but not before yet another accident proved almost fatal.

Bowers suddenly fell down a crevasse. He was out of sight and was held up partly by his sledging harness. Wilson secured this while Cherry-Garrard got the Alpine rope ready. He crawled to the edge of the crevasse and peered down.

'Make a bowline for my foot', shouted Bowers.

This Cherry-Garrard did and lowered the rope. Then

with one foot in the bowline Bowers was inch by inch hauled up again. They were tired men and the temperature was minus 46 degrees, so they were not anxious for any more crevasses to fall into.

Pitching camp under such conditions is not a pleasant job. Here is an account of how it was done.

"We gradually got the buckles undone, and spread the green canvas floor-cloth on the snow. Our next job was to lift our three sleeping-bags one by one on to the floor-cloth; they covered it, bulging over the sides —those obstinate coffins which were all our life to us. Taking a pole in each hand we three spread the bamboos over the whole. We lowered them gently on to the soft snow, that they might not sink too far. Then over with the outer cover, and for one of us the third worst job of the day was to begin. The worst job was to get into our bags; the second was to lie in them for six hours; this third worst was to get the primus lighted and a meal on the way."

So day after day they struggled on. "And we *did* stick it. And we kept our tempers." As Captain Scott wrote: "That they should have persisted in this effort in spite of every adversity for five full weeks is heroic. It makes a tale for our generation which I hope may not be lost in the telling."

It was at the beginning of August that at long last they sighted the Winter Hut. And Wilson gave his last order. "Spread out well, and they will be able to see that there are three men."

So ended one of the worst journeys in the world, and the eggs were at length brought back to England, but only by Cherry-Garrard, for Wilson and Bowers sleep in that tent with Scott out on the frozen Antarctic.

Their companion on that winter journey wrote of them: "These two men went through the Winter Journey and lived; later they went through the Polar Journey and died. They were gold, pure, shining, unalloyed. Words cannot express how good their companionship was. Through all those days, the worst I suppose in their dark severity that men have ever come through alive, no single hasty or angry word passed their lips. When, later, we were sure, so far as we can be sure of anything, that we must die, they were cheerful.... It is hard that often such men must go first when others far less worthy remain."